How to
Be Happy
Where You Are

Michelle McKinney Hammond

HARVEST HOUSE PUBLISHERS

EUGENE, OREGON

Published in association with the literary agency of Alive Communications, Inc., 7680 Goddard Street, Suite 200, Colorado Springs, CO 80920. www.alivecommunications.com

Cover photo © Comstock Images / Comstock / Thinkstock

Cover design by Koechel Peterson & Associates, Inc., Minneapolis, Minnesota

HOW TO BE HAPPY WHERE YOU ARE
Copyright © 2012 by Michelle McKinney Hammond
Published by Harvest House Publishers
Eugene, Oregon 97402
www.harvesthousepublishers.com

Library of Congress Cataloging-in-Publication Data
    McKinney Hammond, Michelle.
    How to be happy where you are / Michelle McKinney Hammond.
        p. cm. —(Matters of the heart series)
    ISBN 978-0-7369-3792-4 (pbk.)
    ISBN 978-0-7369-4214-0 (eBook)
    1. Christian women—Religious life. 2. Happiness—Religious aspects—Christianity. 3. Shunammite woman (Biblical figure). I. Title.
    BV4527.M4183 2012
    248.8'43—dc23
                                                    2011033506

To all my sisters who have cried rivers onto their pillows. To those who have caught sparks of hope then released them because they burned their fingers. To those who have finally gotten their heart's desire. To those who have tasted their dream only to find it bitter after the sweetness dissipated. To those who are still waiting...

I pray that God will meet you and settle your questions, quiet your hearts, and fill your souls to overflowing with Himself. That the peace of God that passes all understanding will hold you tight and warm you like a blanket as you shiver in expectation. Remember, my sister, He knows the plans He has for you, and they are better than your own. Feast on that promise, and let it fill you.

Acknowledgments

I almost feel redundant saying this, but I have to thank all the usual suspects at Harvest House. You have championed me through some fierce storms and extreme circumstances. I am so happy I am part of a family who continues to take care of business but also nurtures relationship. It is so rare in this day and age. You truly glorify God—yes, you give an accurate reflection of His faithfulness and love, and I am forever grateful.

To all of you who put up with me (you know who you are) during a time of tremendous trauma and transition. God has once again proven Himself faithful through your support, patience, and love.

Dave Koechel, thanks for being a wonderful friend and listening.

Jesus, I love You. Thank You for writing my story over and over again in Your Word to encourage me and let me know I am not alone.

Contents

Our True Wealth

"Fulfillment." One word with huge implications. To be full. To be filled to the full. To be so full you feel filled. Filled with whatever your deepest longing was. Oh, it sounds simple enough, and yet this one thing eludes so many. If asked what it would take to feel fulfilled, most would take wild stabs in the dark, guessing what would make them get to a place where they would want nothing more. Others would shrug their shoulders, resigned to the truth that they really don't know.

Some people would insist they know exactly what it would take. But upon grasping it, they find themselves in a state of dismay, wondering, *Is this it? Is this all there is to life? Why am I not happy yet? What will it really take to silence this "wanting" within me?* Someone once said it is not the moments of excitement that test our character. No, it is the mundane moments when nothing of great significance is taking place.

How we handle the silence. The sameness. The vast yawn between nothing and anything happening.

And what do we do with all those unrealized desires? Do we just suck it up and make the best of it? Do we question God until we get an answer? Do we make peace with the seeming impossibilities in our lives? And exactly how would we do that, you ask? "Is it possible?" is the greater question. The Word of God tells us that "godliness with contentment is great gain" (1 Timothy 6:6). That our true wealth lies in our ability to be satisfied, as the apostle Paul wrote, in whatever state we find ourselves in.

For those of us who are followers of Christ, there is a great sense of guilt when we face the fact that we are not content, not fulfilled, not as joyful as we think we ought to be. We walk in fear of insulting God, of seeming ungrateful; yet the truth is the truth. We feel this way in spite of walking by faith. And yet it must be noted that part of maturing is making peace with where we presently are. With where we are not. With what we presently have as well as what we don't have. With what we have achieved and what we have not achieved.

Walking through life with open hands, demanding nothing while expecting everything from the hand of God, quiets our hearts because we believe in something even greater than our desires. But where is the path that leads us there? It is before us, but truly it is a journey we take one step at a time. It is the accumulation of our experiences with God that builds trust and silences our questions. Somewhere along the way we let go, allowing Him to put in and take out of our lives whatever He pleases. We rest in the assurance that His timing is perfect. We know that out of His great love He ultimately does what is best for us. He allows and disallows what He will.

As time passes and we mature, we also learn to appreciate God's pacing. We come to understand there is a season for everything. Just as He set the sun, moon, and stars in place to relegate not only light but the earth's calendar, His order rules in our lives. Yes, we make plans, but the Lord's will prevails. He decides the when, the where, and the how. Learning to embrace each season with the assurance that surely it will change affords us the luxury of remaining present and focused on what is before us right now.

All this and more we will explore as we draw a map that will take us from our place of wanting to an oasis called "fulfillment." Yes, it does exist, and it is not as elusive as you might think. In fact, it is a matter of perspective. So, my dear sister, pull up a chair. We're going to start our journey with an old story that isn't so old after all.

That is what I love about the Word of God. As I study the stories in the Old and New Testaments, I never fail to find myself wandering through the pages. My emotions, my desires, my questions, my wrestling matches with God are mirrored in His Word. I find friends who have traveled the way that I am going. I learn from their experiences. I know if I could have conversations with them they would tell me much more than what is written. I imagine their thoughts and reactions and read the script between the lines of black type on white paper that convey their stories.

Such a story is that of the Shunammite woman found in 2 Kings, chapter 4, beginning at verse 8. This is the story of a woman who, like so many of us, has learned to live with what she's been given. Yet the deep yearning of her heart is there, buried under layers of distractions that pose as acceptance. Her story is one of longings, longings realized, longings lost, and then longings recovered.

This woman's life reveals why it is so important to claim contentment *where we are.* Things change. Even when we get what we want, we can lose them quickly, letting them take our joy and peace with them. It is only when we know the true key to contentment that our fulfillment will not waver regardless of circumstances. This is where I pray that all our hearts will rest. So let's glean from our Old Testament sister, the Shunammite woman, together, shall we? Hopefully we, like her, will find that fulfillment is not so distant a dream after all.

PART 1

Where Are You?

As foolish as it may sound, asking "Where are you?" is a good question. Before any GPS, no matter how sophisticated it may be, can give us directions to where we want to go, it has to lock in on where we are presently in order to plan a route to our desired destination. Sometimes it is hard for us to know where we are. I once found myself in unfamiliar surroundings in a foreign place, so I called someone on the phone for directions. The person asked, "Where are you?" To which I replied, "I have no idea." The person was not able to help me. She had nothing to work with.

God sometimes asks us the same question. Not because He doesn't know the answer, but because He wants us to know the answer. We can only be as honest with God as we are with ourselves. Transparency and truth are the forerunners to victory in our lives. Repeatedly the Word of God emphasizes the need for confession. I've said this often: God will not address what we will not confess. He is a gentleman waiting for us to bring Him our needs, no matter how small, no matter how shameful, no matter how great.

The catalyst for us arriving at our desired destination is our willingness to admit where we are presently as well as being clear about where we want to go. No distraction in the world will ever permanently erase the longings of our hearts.

It is far better to be honest and realistic about where we are in order to gain perspective on where we stand. So you are single. Today. So you are in financial straits. Today. So your marriage is on the rocks. Today. So your dreams are unfulfilled. Today.

Yes, today. God knows what tomorrow holds. He knows the plans He has for you. The problem for us is that He doesn't always let us know what He is planning. He keeps the blessings He has stored up for us under His divine protection lest they be exposed and aborted.

So while we get real about where we are, don't let it cancel out the expectation of going beyond where we presently stand. Our present is the stepping stone to our future, but it is not the end all. As someone once said, it's not over 'til the fat lady sings. But I say for the believer, it's *never* over! Eternity awaits when we've finished our work on this earth. Every circumstance in our lives feeds into an eternal picture that has so much more to do with where we are going than where we are today.

In God's economy of time, a day is as a thousand, and He has all the time in the world to work out His purposes in us and through us. For us, the perspective is vastly different because we feel we are victims of time—manipulated and held captive. Time is running out! We haven't accomplished all that we had hoped. There is an urgency tied to our search for fulfillment that has to do with completion. We feel unfinished. And yet Jesus said, "It is finished." He finished everything that needed to be finished at Calvary to purchase our completion. As we take a look not only at where we are, but where God ultimately wants to take us, His Holy Spirit, who abides in us, bridges the gap to lay a foundation for us to rest upon.

As we seek contentment we also need to rest. To rest in God's timing. To let Him work out the intricacies of our lives and fill us to overflowing with Himself. As we rest in the wholeness that comes from Him—and Him alone—we find the path to completion…and the joy of continuing to walk in it day by day. We walk with open hands that don't feel empty because God is constantly filling them with good and perfect things according to the day and our present needs. In quiet and confidence of God's goodness, we find strength and wholeness, which is really what fulfillment is all about. No gaps, no voids, no room for chaos. No need for questions. It is well with our souls. This too takes time to move from our heads to our hearts.

So for today, we will begin where we are and move forward. Step by step we grow through and past our experiences until we arrive at a place beyond our wildest dreams. This place God has prepared for us as we follow after Him, dragging our questions with us. He is not afraid of them. Neither is He put off when we tell Him where we are. He can handle it. As a matter of fact, He can't wait for us to get real with Him so He can reveal all that He is willing and able to do in our lives. He is waiting to transform and transport us beyond where we are right now. But it begins with us coming out of denial. Removing all the props and distractions and baring our souls. "Yes," He says, "let's talk—but only if you are willing to keep it real. Cast your cares on Me because I care for you."

So, you're not sure where to begin? Let's begin with where you are.

Keeping Up Appearances

One day Elisha went to Shunem. And a well-to-do woman was there, who urged him to stay for a meal (2 Kings 4:8).

❧

It was an ordinary day, quite like every other. The sun rose as it did every morning. She could hear the movements of others. Water being poured into basins. Sounds from the road as people headed to their places of business. She rose early, going about her usual tasks. Nothing different; the same routine. After rising and spending some time meditating, saying her prayers, and making her petitions to God, she turned her eyes from the spiritual to the natural.

She made her list of things to do for the day and checked it twice. It was up to her to call her household to order—giving her servant girls their various tasks, making sure breakfast was being made for her husband, sitting with him as they prepared for the day. At his departure, she too set out on her way. Now her day was really beginning.

She was a prominent woman in the community. A woman of means and great reputation. She enjoyed the privileges of the life she had made for herself. Reaching out her hands to the needy, she was charitable and kind. She reaped the friendships of many because of what she invested in the lives of others.

She was settled. Life with her husband was peaceful and good. She really had no complaints. She lived well. Yes, it was accurate to say that she looked good "on paper," as some would say. From the outside looking in, she had it all.

Of course, there were some who would beg to differ. They would point out that she had no children. And hers was a society that placed a lot of stock in what a woman was able to produce. Was she a vine bearing the fruit of many children? This was considered *true* wealth, an economic plus. So though she was wealthy in material things and the trappings of life, when it came to children she was impoverished. Yes, some people would have pitied her, but they would do so silently, not wanting to ruffle the feathers of all who thought well of her.

She was known for being benevolent, and this went a long way to redeem her among her peers. If she ever compared herself to other women and sorrowed at her childlessness, no one knew. She always seemed serene and at peace with her lot in life. She busied herself helping others without a thought to herself.

This day, even as she made her way on such an appointment, something distracted her. A voice drew her from her path, causing her to halt and listen. There he stood in the center of town talking. A man. A prophet called Elisha. He was expounding on the things of God.

As she drew nearer to hear his words, something deep within her stirred. Her soul seemed to open its mouth to drink in everything he was saying. The more he spoke, the more her hunger grew for more. Yes, more. This was an unfamiliar yet familiar feeling...this wanting more. More of what, she didn't know. She only knew she could no longer live life as it had been. She could no longer accept things at face value. She could no longer be satisfied with what had satisfied her before. She wanted more.

Long after most of the crowd dispersed, she still stood nearby, waiting for him to say more. When more was not forthcoming, she moved forward, inviting him to join her for a meal. Perhaps as they broke bread together he would tell her more. More of whatever it would take to fill the void within her. Yes, his words would fill what a meal could not.

She forgot the scheduled appointment as she led him to her home. Her first departure from the norm. Suddenly the day was quite different. It had taken a turn from ordinary to extraordinary. Deep within she felt the expectancy that more was in store. Exactly what, she wasn't sure, but she would see. Yes, she would see...

I too have felt the void that seems to yawn endlessly within. A divine discomfort. I can't quite put my finger on what I want. All I know is that I want more. More out of life. More than what is before me. This feeling comes and goes. I am able to shake it off, smoosh it down, and get on with my life. But then quiet moments come, and the longing returns like an old familiar friend, reminding me that he is still here, striving for attention, beckoning me to embrace him again. I have felt this longing in different stages in my life. I am sure no one, with the exception of my closest friends, would guess that my life is not so perfect after all. Perhaps the same is true of you.

We also can look good on the outside. Yet something lurks behind the cover of our perfect facades. For this reason alone I have ceased to envy others. We never know what's really going on with them unless they tell us. I can attest that even in the midst of having a glamorous career, flying all over the country, hobnobbing with the elite, being on the "A-list," eating in the best restaurants, living with no financial worries, I sometimes found myself wondering why I wasn't fulfilled. Yes, my life looked great to others. They thought I was living "the life of Riley" with nary a care. How could I tell them it wasn't all that? That something was missing? However, I didn't know what "it" was.

I felt guilty for even daring to think that all I had was not enough. And yet it really wasn't. I wanted something more. Something different. I longed for a shift to take place in my life. For something to occur that would give my life meaning. Yes, my work was creative and exciting. Yes, I got to meet fascinating people. Yes, I got to see the world through a privileged lens. But it all could seem so empty at times. Where was the profit emotionally and spiritually, the deep satisfaction, the lasting contentment, the consistent happiness?

Oh, there were moments when I felt a great sense of satisfaction, but usually they were moments that had nothing to do with my work. My work simply afforded me the moment. To listen to an actor or model's heart and share the love of God. Or the times I could apply scriptural principles to people's lives to help them solve their dilemmas. That would light me up. That would be a day when I felt I had done something that mattered. I had given someone something precious—hope.

Small wonder Jesus could say with assurance when questioned by the disciples about His lack of hunger after a transforming encounter with a woman at a well: "'I have food to eat that you know nothing about…My food,' said Jesus, 'is to do the will of him who sent me'" (John 4:32,34). That's it. We all exist for a greater purpose than going through the motions of life to get from point A to point Z. Life is more than a paycheck or even what we acquire. It is about the moments when we make a difference in the lives of others. The occasions when we get past ourselves and, instead, pour ourselves out for the betterment of another person or cause—in those moments we tap into God and His kingdom agenda. That's when we fulfill the reason we were created. Fulfillment overtakes us and floods our souls with joy. I've said it often: Success in life can never be measured by what we achieve and what we acquire. It is measured by who others become because of our presence.

For me, fulfillment was based on God's call to ministry. For you it could be His call to marriage, motherhood, or some cause that fills your heart with a deep longing to make a positive change. I believe the deepest longings in our hearts are also God's deepest longings for us. We are in right relationship with God, we are completely in sync, our desires cannot be compartmentalized. The Word clearly tells us that if we delight in God, He will give us the desires of our hearts (Psalm 37:4). Yes, the things we thought we wanted are transformed into His desires when we draw closer to Him. And we cannot fully be at rest until we fulfill the request—the call—of God's heart for our lives. The intangibles complete us. Giving ourselves away, being truly significant, establishing our identities in Christ—in something greater than anything we can physically touch—that's what creates contentment.

This brings to mind a year I found myself in California. I was unemployed, broke, and on the verge of losing my apartment. I shut myself in to have a conversation with God about it. With heavy heart and anxiety about my circumstances, I pressed my way into His presence. I began to worship Him. In the midst of my worship, I sensed a change in the atmosphere. I felt overtaken by God's presence. In that profound moment I heard Him clearly ask me, "What do you want?" My mind did a scan of the list of things I felt I needed. But suddenly the list seemed insignificant in His presence. So though I needed money, a job, direction on what to do next, I could only utter, "I need more of You, God. More of You…"

I realized at the core of my soul that if I could be filled to overflowing with God's Spirit, all the other issues would be settled. I would know what to do, and He would lead me to an oasis of supply. In that moment, relief flooded over me. I knew everything would be all right as I shifted my focus to where I was with God. And it was true. Everything I needed fell into place after that. All it took was a change of my priorities.

Perhaps today you feel such a longing. Or perhaps you've numbed it, dumbed it down, found ways to distract yourself from what your soul secretly cries out for. Perhaps you've settled for looking good on the outside. God won't let you stay there. He will send someone to stand in the square of your heart and speak words that press all your buttons and remind you there is still something more. God wants to give you more, and He will not allow you to wallow in denial. Neither will He allow you to remain in a place of wanting. So stop, listen, and prepare to receive...

Hunger Pangs

- What was the one thing you thought would complete you the most—but hasn't?
- In what ways have you felt robbed or denied?
- How has this lack affected your outlook on life?
- What have you done to deal with this sense of lack?
- What would change in your life if you received your desire?

Food for Your Soul

God wants to be actively involved in bringing our fulfillment to pass. Small wonder He promises that He is the rewarder of those who diligently seek Him. He goes on to say that He is our great and exceeding reward, and at His right hand are pleasures evermore (Genesis 15:1; Psalm 16:1). He factors Himself into our ultimate sense of fulfillment. What He says is that when we find ourselves surrounded by Him, we will also find everything else we are looking for. God is definitely the beginning of the path to what we are searching for. And in Him our searching ends. We rest in who He is, what He is able to do, and in His divine timing. But most of all, we can rest in the fact that He is God.

Initial Hunger

*So whenever [Elisha] passed that way, he would
turn in there to eat food* (2 Kings 4:8 ESV).

🪶

She looked forward to the prophet Elisha's visits. The time always
seemed to pass too quickly when he came for dinner. She was
thankful he made the time to dine with her and her husband every
time he passed through town. She came to anxiously wonder when he
would come again. And then, as if in answer to the prayer in her heart,
he would return. From the moment he entered the house the atmosphere changed. Vitality invaded her soul, a sharp contrast to the rest
of her days that were so filled with activity there was little time for feeling anything. This was when she realized that perhaps her busyness
was a distraction to veil the sameness of her existence. This had never
occurred to her until Elisha's visits started. The excitement she felt

when he arrived had been missing for quite some time. How long, she really couldn't remember. All she knew was that she reveled in conversations with him, hanging on his every word. His words filled her soul and the feast they partook of filled her stomach. But she knew it was the prophet's wisdom from God that made her feel so energized. She felt as if she would burst. And after he left, the fullness lingered.

Then hunger would come. And it unearthed other hungers that had lain dormant. The pangs surprised her, stirring up longings within she thought she had long put to rest. She averted her attention from them. After all, she really had no right to want anything. She had a wonderful life. A loving husband. A great home. The freedom to follow her passions. Good standing in her community. She had no health issues. No financial worries. No, she had nothing to complain about—especially when she looked around her. There were people who had great struggles. Deep troubles. All manner of problems. She sometimes felt guilty that her life was so good. She kept quiet when listening to the trials and tribulations of others, being reticent about giving her own praise report lest she appear insensitive. She almost felt sorry about being so blessed in light of the woes of others.

She also didn't want to appear ungrateful to God. She kept silent about the hunger within. When it returned, she intensified her service to those in need. She turned her focus to praising God for what He had done in her life. These were exercises in reminding herself why she should be content, but still hunger crept from behind her worship. It tapped insistently on the shoulder of her heart, reminding her of its presence.

Then Elisha would come, speaking about God as they broke bread together. His words were like succulent meat for her soul. The more she ingested, the more she wanted. This spiritual food filled her in a way she couldn't describe. She knew she needed it. The charitable works and all the good things she did for others fed her in a different way. They couldn't fill this spot that seemed beyond human reach, like an itch she couldn't scratch.

She lived for those days when she saw him making his way to her house. She often went to the roof to search the horizon for a glimpse of him traveling across the valley and up the road to her village. On the days she spied him, she would quickly instruct the household servants to make ready for his arrival. Even as she created their menu for dinner, she wondered what fare she would enjoy this time round. Elisha's words were a meal in itself. She found that she didn't eat much at their meal, so busy was she taking in his offerings of God's wisdom.

Long after they retired for the night, she would lie awake, meditating on what the prophet had said. Yes, it was rich fare. Eventually she would drift into a satiated sleep, his words filling her dreams. In these times she was full…lacking nothing…a feeling she wanted to keep.

There are days when the sameness of life can lull us into a place of apathy. Not in the negative sense, but in a quiet acceptance of where we are and what we have. We cease to expect anything other than what we are presently experiencing, coming to the conclusion that what we have is all life holds. This is when God comes, stirring and awakening us to what I call "divine discomfort." He will never let us settle into the place where we are because He is constantly moving forward with His kingdom agenda. Like a mother bird stirring up her nest and encouraging her brood to stretch their wings and fly, God comes to unsettle us. To awaken us. To stimulate our hunger for something more.

What we do with this God-inspired hunger affects our destiny. Attitude is everything. We always have options, whether we think we do or not. We can complain about our station in life and all that comes with it. We can magnify the negative until we see no positives at all. We can allow a bad attitude to cause us to seek the wrong things to abate our hunger. Or we can use every void to create a new opportunity. We can find ways to magnify the positives until they overtake the negatives. We can choose to make the right choices despite how we feel until we are overtaken by the peace God gives.

God has clearly said that we do not live by bread alone but by every word that proceeds from His mouth (Matthew 4:4). God anticipates our hunger and makes daily provision for us. He waits for us to invite Him to dinner. As we feast on Him, He fills the empty spaces in our lives, satisfying us. But He always leaves enough space so our hunger for Him will return.

I've discovered that when I am ready to draw closer to God and open myself to new possibilities that build on fulfilling His desire for me, my hunger for Him builds. It begins as a faint niggling sensation, almost as if I have a tapeworm in the pit of my stomach. A spiritual need that mimics a physical one. I can't quite put my finger on what I'm hungry for; I am only aware of my need for something more than what I have. This is a critical point. What I do with my hunger will impact my attitude, my health, my emotions…my life.

I can opt to fill up on junk in the form of food or senseless activity. This will satisfy for a moment, distracting me from what God wants me to discover…the point He wants to make…the sustenance He wants to provide that will help me grow strong. Or I can choose to be still and seek God's counsel for direction, for what He wants me to turn my attention to.

There have been times when I've felt empty and satiated myself with shopping, spending on nonessentials and using my charge cards, only to regret the bill I created later. I've filled up on junk food, getting on a roll by devouring sweets and foods that threaten my cholesterol level and ability to fit into my present wardrobe. Can you relate? Our hunger can cause us to pursue things that lead to greater lack. And then there we are, asking God to bless us and get us out of our mess once again.

The danger for making wrong choices increases when we feel our options are limited or nonexistent. Ever notice that when you decide to go on a diet you are always hungry? Always thinking about food? If we allow ourselves to fall for the trick in the garden that Eve succumbed to, we may believe God is holding out on us so we choose to take matters into our own hands. To satisfy our longings our own way. This independence is our statement that God isn't enough, that He won't provide. We lose more than we ever imagine every time we take this stance.

Behind the question posed to Adam and Eve, "Who told you that you were naked?" was the deeper question: "Who told you that you needed more than I have already provided for you?" Truly, if every good and perfect gift comes from God, and He has promised to provide everything we need, then we already have available everything that is healthy, fulfilling, and beneficial. At any moment in time, we only need to ask God to help us embrace and celebrate what He has already given us. When we do this, He comes, opening our hearts and preparing us to receive more of what He wants to give us.

I believe the Bible is not all God knows. I think He shares what He knows we need and what we can handle. When we ask, He will help us get to the place where we can receive His wisdom. And each time we grow and ask for more, He will give us even greater blessings because now we are able to appreciate and maintain them.

We need to be careful what we do with our hunger. We don't want to allow it to dictate our actions or change our attitude toward God. It's safe to say that the Shunammite woman was not aware of the intensity of her hunger when she first invited the man of God to dinner. She just knew Elisha had something she wanted. Little did she know her longing was a setup to even greater blessing.

Hunger Pangs

- In what areas of your life have you settled in to sameness?
- What parts of your daily life are matters of habit rather than results of passionate desire?
- Do you feel God is purposefully withholding something from you? If so, explain.
- In what ways do you try to satisfy your hunger? What activities are more distraction than seeking God's purpose?
- What is God's purpose for the hunger you feel right now?

Food for Your Soul

When you are wanting, rest assured that God will not leave you that way. The Lord is your shepherd. You shall not want or lack any good thing. He will lead you to places of supply and fulfillment beyond your deepest longing. Resist the temptation to graze on things that lead you away from the promise of His supply and blessing. Remember that your desire will always be smaller than what He has in store for you. He is truly able to do exceedingly beyond what you can ask or think (see Psalm 23).

Keeping Good Company

She said to her husband, "Behold now, I know that this is a holy man of God who is continually passing our way. Let us make a small room on the roof...so that whenever he comes to us, he can go in there" (2 Kings 4:9-10).

꙳

S he watched him gather his things after dinner and prepare to take his leave. It had been a rich evening. It just didn't seem right for him to seek lodging elsewhere after such a life-changing time in her home. No, it just didn't seem right. He had become like family. They greeted one another warmly upon meeting. She enjoyed feeding him and serving him, counting it a privilege that he would choose to spend any of his time with her. He was patient to answer her questions, never making her feel as if anything she asked was foolish. She realized she was drawn to him not just because of what he knew. No, she also knew he cared about her, about her husband, about their well-being.

She'd always chosen her friends well, realizing that people are the company they keep. She kept her circle small and containable, choosing to focus on investing richly into the lives of those she chose to walk with. She knew there was a difference between friends and associates. She went to extra measures to be present in her close relationships. She felt close to this man…this man of God. This was what she had come to realize above all things about her special guest. He was not like some of the religious men she had observed. They were all talk with no love, compassion, or integrity. They always had a hand out, making empty promises that never came to pass. But this one was different. He was truly a prophet and man of God in word and deed. His demeanor betrayed a passion for God that she liked. He made her feel comfortable. Comfortable enough to open their doors to him and invite him to stay. Perhaps if he stayed longer the anointing on his life would saturate their own. She longed to feel and experience God the way he did. To have firsthand knowledge of the power of God. When Elisha was near she felt closer to achieving that goal.

She prayed her husband would feel the same way and agree to make him more than a guest. After all he had given to them, it was the least they could do to show their appreciation. For all he had sown into their lives, it was time for them to sow into his. As for her, she would not be guilty of taking without giving. As a matter of fact, this is what made her come to life. She loved pouring love into the lives of others, serving their needs with abandon. This was when she experienced her greatest joy. And she couldn't think of anyone else she would rather share her home with other than her husband…and God. She laughed. Perhaps having Elisha here was the same as inviting God to stay!

I recall the first time I saw my cousin, a famous bishop from Africa, speak at a church. As he walked across the stage, people standing in the congregation fell to the floor, so great was the power of God. The bishop spoke and divulged so much revelation knowledge about prayer that it changed my approach to prayer and transformed my life. I decided that day I wanted what he had. I wanted to know God in such a way that His power would touch people around me in profound and life-changing ways.

I asked my cousin if I could serve him. Just as bad company can corrupt good manners, I knew that great company could make me better. No errand was beneath me. I was so excited to be in his presence and associated with what he was doing that I went the extra mile to be a blessing to him. I knew the more I did, the more he was free to be effective for the kingdom of God. Yes, I was earning gems for my heavenly crown I would use to honor Jesus, but I was also learning spiritual things I would learn no other way (2 Timothy 4:8; James 1:12; Revelation 4:10). I learned by the bishop's example. It was mentorship at its best. He would constantly correct me because nothing escaped his vision as I walked with him daily. His watchfulness birthed greater character in me and helped me develop deeper spiritual understanding.

After a while I began to come into my own. His inspiration had become a manifestation in my life. I liken it to how the disciples of Jesus mirrored what Jesus did while on earth. And Jesus, of course, mirrored His heavenly Father. We become a reflection of the company we keep. My advice is that if you want something positive to happen in your life, hang out with people who are successful at what you aspire to do.

The Shunammite woman knew Elisha had something she wanted. The intimacy he had with God and His anointing was missing from her life. She felt the difference when this man of God came into her presence. She knew it was his connection with God that set him apart. She also knew that to glean the full benefit of her relationship with him, short visits would not be enough. She needed extended quality time to absorb the fullness of who he was and what he shared.

The same is true of us with God. Short visits will never suffice. It is the daily time spent with Him, the sustained time spent in His presence. A consistent walk with God will fill us and ultimately bear fruit in our lives. This deliberate delight in serving Him flows into the empty spaces in our lives and rearranges our priorities and perspectives on all we hold dear and desire. Yes, our desires change! We will walk with our hands open to His service more and more as we walk in expectancy of the goodness of God and the manifestation of His power. We do have a choice when it comes to the company we keep, and that company affects our mindset.

Like the paralyzed man lying by the pool of Bethesda in John, chapter 5, we too can become immobile and cease to hope for more if the people around us have settled into the mindset that "this is all life holds" or "that's just the way it is." If that is all we see, that is all we will get... until we meet someone who is larger than life, who ignites our imagination and our faith, who awakens a sense of daring to stretch our beliefs and see what God sees. If faith comes by hearing, we must be selective in who we are listening to. Our conversations impact our attitudes and actions. No matter where we are in life, we need to be aware of the influence of the company we choose to keep.

Hunger Pangs

- Consider your three closest relationships. How do they positively and negatively influence your life?
- How much do your conversations with these people affect your mindset or attitude?
- What do you typically focus on when you grow discontent?
- What gives you hope in those moments?
- Do you need to make a shift in your thinking? If so, what shift, and how will you do this?
- How will your current relationships help or hinder your desire to change?

Food for Your Soul

God uses divine discomfort in our lives to create openings for the furtherance of His plan and to get us to be open to the new things He wants to do in our lives and in the lives of the people around us. Satan tries to duplicate that God-given unrest or dis-ease, but he can only stir up discontent. He points his finger to what God hasn't done in our lives and suggests that God is withholding blessings from us.

Have you experienced that? In those moments, may I suggest that you not respond? Do not enter into a discussion or debate with the enemy of your soul. Your response to the spiritual hunger within you will be guided by the company you keep. Choose your dinner guest carefully. Choose the One who has promised that when invited in, He will sup with you and nourish your soul with life-giving conversation. With soul food that is delicious and nutritious. With heart food that will make you strong in Him. Be still and know that He is God. Seek Him. Invite Him in. Dine with Him. Revel in His good company. Entertain Him and Him alone, lest you plummet to a place of despair. He is the only dinner guest who promises to fill you to overflowing and satisfy your hunger, your thirst, and your desires above and beyond your expectations.

PART 2

Where Is God?

In moments of discontent we must deal with one huge question: Is God good or not? After all, where is He as we seek solace and satisfaction by wandering endlessly through the chambers of our longings? The answer? He is right here. Waiting patiently until we see Him. He has promised to be the rewarder of those who diligently seek Him. He will be our great and exceeding reward! At His right hand are pleasures evermore (Hebrews 11:6; Genesis 15:1; Psalm 16:1). That sounds so good, but how realistic is it in light of what we want while living on this earth now?

It is as real as our capacity to believe and acknowledge that God is good. To walk in a healthy fear, which translates as "reverent wonder and submission," opens the door to experiencing the best God has to offer. We anticipate His goodness and make room for it. This is where God meets all who believe in Him and His Son, Jesus Christ, and shows us greater manifestations of Himself.

This reminds me of the parable of the three servants who were given money before their master set off on a long trip. He had dispensed the talents according to what he knew they could handle. God loves us so much He is protective even in how He gives gifts. He only gives us what He knows we can handle. Just as He lovingly escorted Adam and Eve out of the Garden of Eden lest they live forever in their sinful state, He disallows some things in our lives that may look good to us because He knows the far-reaching implications of every acquisition. Consider the tender mercy of God withholding what we think we desire. He stays true to His Word that His blessings make us rich and add no sorrow to our lives. In this light, we can see every "prevention," every "no," as an act of protection. But when He is ready to add something to our lives He makes room for it and gives us the capacity to receive it and to maintain and sustain the blessing as well.

How many times have we longed for things and wondered why we didn't get them? The answer lies in this simple story.

In Matthew 25, we read about Jesus telling the parable of a master who gives his servants talents according to their abilities. He gave one servant five talents, another servant three, and the last servant one. In the end, the master's wisdom was proven correct as the two servants with the most money did well with what they received, investing wisely and presenting the profit to their master upon his return. But the third servant, who had been given only one talent, buried his and had nothing more to share than what he had originally been given.

When the master asked for an accounting, the third servant explained his lack of motivation away by shifting blame to the master, citing he was a hard man who had far too much access to undeserved gain. The servant was afraid of the master, and so he was paralyzed from doing anything above and beyond the call of duty.

This servant withheld his service, his respect, and his honor. The master called him wicked and lazy and took away the original talent he had been given. He gave it to one of the other workers who had proven to be productive and fruitful.

Then the master applauded the other two who had done well and promised that those who had been fruitful would be given more, but the ones who had not been productive would suffer the loss of even the little they already had. The moral of the story? Perception is what will inspire and enable us to make the best of what we have been given.

Our view of God will either incite an expectation of greater things or disappointment.

If we truly expect great things from God our approach to life is one of actively living out our gratitude by having a healthy approach to the daily routine of life. Gratitude makes room for further blessing because it helps us stay always expectant. Always looking for ways to thank God for what He has already done while trusting Him for more as He deems fit. On the flip side, dissatisfaction is paralyzing. It cuts off our hope and allows us to make excuses for not living better lives, for not doing what is required to take us to the next level in spiritual maturity. We feel depleted and drained. Too empty to pursue the blessings God wants to give.

Perhaps this is why He promises in quiet and confidence shall be our strength. It is our confidence in His love for us, along with His desire for the best for us, that gives us the strength to wait joyfully with an attitude of gratitude that is energizing.

You've heard the mantra "God is good all the time." Did you wonder about it? Well, it is true! Every good and perfect gift comes from above—make no mistake about that. God longs to give us good gifts, but He gives only in accordance to our ability to handle them. He focuses on building our character before expanding our grasp.

If we believe God is good, we must come to a place of quiet confidence and trust in His divine timing. As we rest in this place, we are able to wait with full hearts. Instead of gazing longingly at what we lack, we are looking forward to what God has planned for us.

God knows His plans for us—plans for good and wholeness, to give us hope and a future (Jeremiah 29:11). He is just as excited to give as we are to receive. Yes, our God is truly good!

So where is God? Everywhere! He is ever present. Ever holding in His hands blessings for us beyond our imagination.

4

Desires in Perspective

Once when [Elisha] was resting in the room he said to his
servant Gehazi, "Tell the woman I want to speak to her."

When she came, he said to Gehazi, "Tell her that we appreciate her
kindness to us. Now ask her what we can do for her. Does she want me
to put in a good word for her to the king or to the general of the army?"

"No," she replied, "I am perfectly content" (2 Kings 4:11-13 TLB).

༚

When the servant appeared in the doorway her heart leapt.
"My master would like to see you," he said.

"I'll be right there," she answered.

"I'll tell him," Gehazi replied. He turned and quietly headed back
up the stairs.

Suddenly the Shunammite woman felt anxious. This was unusual.
Elisha had never asked her to come to his quarters. Yes, she served him.
They talked long into the evening until her husband began to nod in

his chair, and then the prophet would retire to his room. *Is something wrong? Why does he want to see me?* she wondered. *Have I offended him in some way?* To be called to meet with him in private, apart from her husband, signaled something…she just wasn't sure what.

Wiping her hands nervously on her dress, she climbed the stairs to reach the room on the roof. She remembered when she'd approached her husband about building this special place for the man of God. Her husband had agreed without hesitation, sensing that this visitor in their home was special. They had paid special attention to details, first building the room and then making sure it was furnished in a way that would make Elisha comfortable. She had furnished the room with a bed, a chair, a small table, and a lamp. Of course, Elisha had access to the rest of their home, but this room was his. She wanted him to never feel that he had to rush to leave, that this was his home too. As she made her way to him now, she checked to make sure the steps and surroundings were clean. She wanted everything to be perfect for him.

She took a deep breath when she got to the top of the stairs, again rubbing her hands nervously. Tentatively she knocked. Her stomach knotted when she heard his voice.

"Come in!" Elisha called.

Carefully she stepped just inside the door, then slowly inching forward, stopping short of the center of the room. Elisha was looking at her intently, a gentle smile on his face. This should have relaxed her, but instead she felt even greater trepidation. She always felt as if he saw more than was evident on the surface, especially when she looked into his eyes. They were filled with a knowing that made her shift in discomfort. She felt exposed under his gaze. Not in a bad way. Just bare, open, vulnerable. She wondered if he knew all her secrets. She averted her gaze.

Then he spoke, addressing her through his servant Gehazi, as was the custom: "Tell her that we appreciate her kindness to us. Now ask her what we can do for her. Does she want me to put in a good word for her to the king or to the general of the army?"

She couldn't believe her ears. What was he saying? She hadn't done what she had to garner praise or curry favor. She felt it was a privilege to serve him. She did pray that the anointing that rested on his life would in some way touch her life and empower her to help others the way he did. She wanted to be a blessing in the lives of others. And now he was asking what he could give her in exchange for hosting him in her home? What price could she attach to a situation that made her feel like she was the one left owing?

No, there was nothing he could give her other than what he was already. Her mind did a quick scan of her life. There was nothing she could put her finger on that was missing. For a moment something almost imperceptible within her stirred, but she wasn't sure what it was and didn't comprehend its origin, so she simply shook her head and said, "I am perfectly content."

She was saying she was at home among her people. Her family and friends loved her and she was cared for. She was indeed content. After all, she should be. She was the envy of her friends. Her husband was kind, she had a good home, her health, a good life. She was not left wanting. She had nothing to complain about. Nothing at all…

There is that sweet spot in life that we hit from time to time, when we think to ourselves, *Things can't get any better than this.* For most of us this doesn't last long. This is a natural, up and down cycle of life. I like to call it one-tree-i-tis. The enemy of our souls will always come suggesting that we are missing out on something, just like he did with Adam and Eve on that tragic afternoon in the Garden of Eden. Yes, Satan brings that disease of dissatisfaction that makes us believe God is withholding something we desire. It has a loud voice that pleads with us to take life into our own hands—to do whatever is necessary to achieve or acquire our heart's desire. Ah, but when we are "not wanting," it is such a sweet feeling. And God lets us enjoy that for a while. Then He pushes our buttons and asks us questions to reveal what is hidden in our hearts. He asks questions He already knows the answers to. Why? Because He wants us to be honest with ourselves so that we will be honest with Him.

When we bare ourselves before our loving God, He tenderly reaches out to touch and fill the empty places in our hearts. Many of us wear brave faces. We meet people every day who ask us how we are. We reply with an automatic, "I'm fine." But really we aren't. Our preference is not to reveal ourselves on a deep level in passing conversation, so we suck up our misgivings, tuck in our feelings, and put our best face forward—even if we are really feeling torn up inside or "tore up from the floor up," as some say. In other instances, we are kind of okay. We have nothing specific to complain about, but we know something is missing. We can't identify it, we just know the feeling is present. This is when the Holy Spirit searches our hearts, uncovering the hidden things, exposing them to God, and making intercession for us within the will of our heavenly Father for our lives.

Let's face it, if we've waited for a longing to be fulfilled for a long time, somewhere along the way we resign ourselves to living without that desire coming true. We decide it is time to let go and get on with it. The thought of clinging to our desires and continuing to wonder when they will come to pass becomes too overwhelming and wearying. We decide it's time to forget about it in order to preserve our sanity and any measure of joy we can. It is safe to say we go into survival mode, burying our desire. And yet it remains…whether we acknowledge it or not.

God knows about your desires. This much you need to know. He waits for you to be willing to dare to hope again and bring your desire to Him. He will allow it to lay latent until He deems it the perfect time to bring it to pass.

In a moment when you are neither thinking about it nor looking for it, God will pose a question to your heart: "What can I do for you, my child, my daughter, my love?" In that moment you, like the Shunammite woman, will have to make an assessment of your life. All that you hold and all that you've been privileged to receive. In that moment you would probably say the same thing she did. At the end of the day, life has not been so bad. You are clothed and fed and in your right mind. You're fairly sound in body and have a roof over your head. You eat every day. You have more than most people in the world, so it doesn't feel right to complain. Right? You should be content. But are you?

Is there something off? What is the missing link? At some point in your life perhaps you've buried your desire so deeply that you don't even know what you long for anymore. And yet God does. His purpose and plan for your life continues to incubate within you until the fullness of time when He fills us with what He desires to bring to pass in our lives.

God also waits to see if the thing you desire will become a god to you or if He will remain *the* God in your life. When God is your choice, the resolve of your heart is reflected in these simple words: "I am content. If I never get that desire, I will still praise Him."

These words and attitudes release the hand of God. He can trust you with the blessing. Your desire will not consume you. It will not become a gift that leads to destruction. Your heart has been enlarged to accommodate both the gift and the Giver in the right perspective. Sometimes this can take a while…longer than we realize. But on that day, God will move heaven and earth to bring your desire to pass. This is called dying to self and all you hold dear to make room for the greater plan of the One who loves you most and desires only good and perfect gifts for your life.

Hunger Pangs

- Take inventory of your life. What are the top five things you are grateful for?
- What desire has God most recently fulfilled in your life?
- What desires remain?
- What conclusion have you come to about your unfulfilled desire?
- What would your attitude toward life be if you never received what you longed for? And how about toward God?

Food for Your Soul

God will never give us what He knows will detract from our lives. It is in the quiet confidence that He always has our best interest at heart that we are able to release Him with joyful anticipation to operate according to His divine timing. A very ill friend of mine told me one day that though she anticipated being healed, she had come to the conclusion that if God never did another thing for her, He had already done enough. He had been faithful. She had a life rich in relationships and accomplishments. She had experienced an intimacy with God that filled her to overflowing. And that had truly put all things into perspective. What more could she ask for? God had already given her everything. Anything else could only be considered extra perks. This is life at its fullest.

God's Determination

[Elisha] said, "What then is to be done for her?" Gehazi answered, "Well, she has no son, and her husband is old" (2 Kings 4:14 ESV).

lisha watched her leave the room. He'd heard what this woman had said about being content, but her heart spoke even louder than her words. She was special. He had watched the way she interacted with her help and noted her careful care of him. Seldom had he experienced such sincere generosity. What a blessing was this woman who had humbly come and invited him to dinner. Though she had plenty and was highly regarded in society, there was a sadness about her that would go unnoticed to the undiscerning eye. She was always smiling, yet something in her eyes told him she longed for something beyond her grasp. So attentive was she whenever he stopped by to dine with her that he felt compelled to share all he could. Her grateful attention pulled at his heart, and he longed to fill the void he knew lurked within her.

When he called to ask her what he could do for her, he knew she would never speak the things she harbored deep within. Yet he asked anyway. Her answer confirmed what he'd suspected. Though she said she was content, he knew that was true only on a surface level. He'd suggested general gifts to her because he didn't want her to be uncomfortable. Yes, he could put in a word to the king for extra favor for her and her husband. Of course he could speak to the commander of the army to up their patrols. After all, she and her husband were people of means and the extra protection would always be appreciated. But these things did not get to the heart of the matter. The irony of life was that one could possess so much and yet so little at the same time. Plenty only magnified the lack of the things that were counted truly significant. Yes, it was wonderful to be surrounded by all the trappings that others aspired to possess. But what about the things that satisfy the core of our souls? The things that might be meaningless to others but mean everything to us?

Yes, Elisha knew something was missing from the Shunammite woman's life, but he would not intrude into her personal space. She had been too gracious, kind, and accommodating for him to be insensitive. He sensed a sadness that surfaced only in brief glimpses. She had learned to manage her longings well. Because of how she had pressed past her own desires to attend to his needs, he was determined to be a blessing to her.

He sought God concerning her. Interceding on her behalf. He was careful not to speak out of turn or run ahead of God. People's souls were tender. A person had to be careful before speaking. Being a prophet did not give someone free license to speak at will. He had to be circumspect. It could be a matter of life or death to speak out of turn and be proven wrong. And so he sat, mulling over what he felt he'd heard God say.

Gehazi, his servant, had answered his musing about what could be done for the woman. He confirmed what Elisha had been feeling in his spirit: "a son." That is what this woman wanted. This was a small matter for God. Elisha sensed that the woman had laid the matter to rest in her heart, but her sadness was still apparent. He was not sure if she dared hope once more. But he knew he would deliver joy to her. He had the privilege of letting her know what God intended to do. Would she believe him? No matter. God would prove Himself faithful by honoring the humble service of this woman. Perhaps she was really content to be at home among her people, but God wanted her to be filled to overflowing with blessing. And deep within, Elisha knew she would be.

I believe there is a place in Christ where we don't have to ask God for anything. As we focus on delighting ourselves in Him, He pours out His blessings on us because He refuses to be outdone. If there is any place that God becomes competitive in nature, it is in the area of giving. We cannot out give God in service or worship. He will not be outdone! As we live in Him, His desires become our desires. The things that are not important or conducive to God being glorified fall away, exposing His greater design and desire for our lives.

Because we are passionately connected to Him, His desires burn in our own hearts more and more. At this moment of merging heart and spirit we become pregnant with kingdom purpose. We carry the burden of God's heart and labor to birth it into manifestation. It is our response and attitude during this time of discomfort that compels God to meet us at the area of our deepest need.

God is inspired by our joyful service and worship. When our hearts joyfully surrender to Him, He moves to bless us. God loves cheerful givers. He looks for those who are totally committed to Him in all circumstances. I think of God's affection for Caleb, a protégé of Moses. God said He liked Caleb and would bless him because he followed Him wholeheartedly all his life (Numbers 14:24). For this God rewarded him by allowing Caleb to enter the Promised Land.

Recently after going through a series of very difficult circumstances,

I was distraught. But God proved Himself faithful by restoring all I had lost and more. I lost my home…but inherited two. My business bottomed out, but I inherited two new businesses. Though the companies need a lot of work to restore them to their former prosperity, the potential is there for great profitability. As my friends celebrated what God was doing in my life, they also noted that no matter what I had gone through, as devastating as everything was, I remained hopeful in God, anticipating His blessings. They saw how I praised Him in spite of my disappointment with how my life was going. And they believe God honored my faithfulness.

I, however, hadn't stopped to think about whether I was being faithful to God or not. I felt compelled…I had no choice except to praise Him. Like the Shunammite woman, I felt I could not really complain. I've lived an amazing life. My present circumstances were a mere hiccup in the course of my journey. I dared to believe God would correct my circumstances at some point. I refused to fall prey to my negative feelings or settle into despair. I chose to cling to God and worship Him, trusting Him to turn things around. Where else could I place my faith with such confidence?

At the end of the day, godliness with contentment is great gain (1 Timothy 6:6). It fills the great divide in our hearts and secures our future. God can do amazing things with hearts sold out to Him! He loves to bless those who hope in Him. So hope in this: God is determined to bless you—even if you can no longer voice your desire. He searches your heart and exposes the hidden things, bringing them to light. Yes, He will push your buttons to awaken your heart.

Hunger Pangs

- What is your relationship with God like?
- How open with Him are you about your desires?
- What is the hardest part of living with unfulfilled desires?
- How do you deal with your unresolved longings?
- What about your attitude will encourage God to bless you?

Food for Your Soul

Gratitude is the partner of contentment. We can actively choose to have a conversation with the serpent, the devil, who is anxious to convince us that God is holding out on us, that He's holding wonderful presents behind His back—away from our sight and grasp. Or we can choose to rehearse the list of all we have and what God has done so far in our lives. This is the best witness we can give to the world and to heaven! That we completely trust God with our lives. That we rest in the fact that He delivers only those gifts that are good and perfect... gifts that bring blessing and add no sorrow to our lives.

Hopes Exposed

*"Call her back again," Elisha told [Gehazi]. When the woman
returned, Elisha said to her as she stood in the doorway, "Next
year at this time you will be holding a son in your arms!"*

*"No, my lord!" she cried. "O man of God, don't deceive me
and get my hopes up like that"* (2 Kings 4:15-16 NLT).

She didn't understand why she was being summoned yet again to
Elisha's room. Had her previous answer offended him? She had not
said it to offend. And it was true. Her family and friends took good
care of her. She lacked for nothing. She didn't know what else to say.
Besides, it would have been improper to say anything else. Though
she had invited Elisha into her home, she didn't consider him an intimate friend, the sort she could share her true feelings with. No, she
honored his position and didn't want to abuse the access he granted

her. *Why does he want to see me again? What could I have done that displeased him?* she worried.

She made her way back up the stairs to his room. This time when he called for her to come in she didn't dare enter all the way. She stopped just inside the doorway.

Elisha was seated at the table. He looked intently at her and then said words that would forever change her life: "Next year at this time, you will be holding a son in your arms!"

The Shunammite woman was so shocked she wasn't sure she'd heard him correctly. Had he said she would conceive a child and hold him in her arms next year? How did he know the secret desire of her heart? Now she knew for sure why she always felt he could see into the depths of her soul.

His amazing words shook her to the core. Elation surged…then died. What if what Elisha said didn't come to pass? Sometimes the predictions of prophets were unreliable. When they didn't come true, the prophet was declared to be false—a charlatan. And then the prophet was stoned—killed—as the law instructed. But she knew Elisha was truly a man of God. And since that was true, why would he say such a thing unless he really believed it to be true? Still, it would be cruel to raise such a sensitive issue and have it come to naught. Her hopes had been raised in this area many times, only to come to nothing. She had finally become resigned to the fact that she would never be a mother. It wasn't going to happen. Her husband was older, and she also was getting on in age. Perhaps it was best to put aside the desire for a child, to count her daily blessings and move on with life.

This train of thought had worked most days…that is until she saw a mother with a newborn in her arms. Then it felt like someone stabbed her in the heart. The searing pain of wanting surfaced. She would question again why God hadn't granted this desire of hers. He had provided everything else so richly, but this one thing He had not done. She felt guilty for wanting a child. Perhaps God knew something she didn't, thus His withholding, but she still wanted what she wanted.

So she would talk herself out of the hope once again, tucking away the desire. It was best not to dwell in useless hope. Best not to rehearse a situation she could do nothing about. She should get on with living, putting her hand to what she could and releasing the rest. This gave her peace.

She took a deep breath. This prophet of God, a person she trusted spiritually, was telling her she was going to have a child after all! She didn't know if she should be happy or suspicious. Trusting or angry. Why did he stir up this issue? Suddenly she blurted the words that exposed her heart and hurt: "No, my lord!...O man of God, don't deceive me and get my hopes up like that."

He didn't respond when she said this. Something flickered across his face for a moment, but she couldn't read his expression. He studied her, as if seeing beyond her, as if saying, "You don't have to believe it. I've spoken a Word from the Lord."

The Shunammite turned and fled the room, her heart and thoughts wild with speculation. Should she tell her husband? Would the prophet's words come to pass? Did she dare hope again? No, she wouldn't tell her husband just yet. She would see if this prophecy came to pass. Yes, she would see...

If I'd bought a wedding dress every time someone prophesied to me that I was getting married over the years, I would have amassed a collection large enough to open my own bridal shop! I often say that some people prophalie, prophathink, or prophawish. These prophesies become a very sensitive issue when they're about a desire that's been harbored for a long time.

Can you relate? Someone "prophesies" that you're going to get something you desire. You roll it over in your mind, heart, and imagination for so long that you get weary. For the single person, it might relate to a desire for a husband. For a married person, it might relate to a change in the heart or habits of a mate. Or perhaps it's a more general desire...for a certain dream to come true, a new career, a roomier home. Whatever it is, you're haunted. The prophecy interrupts your joy by wagging unreachable carrots before you. This riveting distraction robs you of the ability to focus on what is before you, what is within reach right now. This unfounded prophecy is a subtle device of the enemy that, if undetected, can rob you of seeing your current blessings.

The struggle to make peace with our desires is an age-old battle. The Bible speaks of it through Paul. He writes to the Philippian church that he is content in all circumstances. In spite of the fact that he has not attained what he would like to, that he has endured many hardships, he has learned to be content in whatever state he finds himself in. Whether full or empty, rich or poor, he is content (Philippians 4:11-12). Why? Because he has faith that God will supply all of his needs. Do his wants make him restless from time to time? Definitely yes. But his needs are settled. Could it be that our needs get mixed up with our wants? And that's when the internal restlessness begins?

I wanted to be married. Did I need to be married? No. Well, at least not until God decides I need to be married. When He makes that decision, I rest assured that marriage will be part of an agenda that goes beyond my personal desire. Then it will be about kingdom business being carried out...kind of like when God decided Adam needed Eve to complete his assignment to multiply. When our hearts and God agree, things happen! Wheels are put into motion, and God grants the desires of our hearts because it is His desire for us too. Our desire becomes His desire as we delight in Him. Voila!

Until then, our search to find a comfortable spot where we are no longer tossed to and fro by our desires can be difficult. It's a hard place to find, but it does exist somewhere between the external pressure of voices telling us what we should have or deserve and our internal assurance that God is in control (based on His Word, which is always true). When we really believe God is in charge, our focus shifts to living in the present. But the temptation is to run ahead or lag behind in our hearts rather than to practice being present, living in the moment and draining all we can from where we are.

God declared His name is "I Am" (Exodus 3:14). The implications behind such a statement are huge. He is literally saying, "I live in the present. Nowhere else. I am not called 'I Was' or 'I Will Be.' No 'I Am.' I am a present God in time of trouble. I dwell in the present. I am here now!" This means listen up and "rack focus." In the world of film, "rack focus" means to adjust the focus, pull it in and clarify your focal point. Get rid of the extraneous and the things that distract from the present scene. In our world this translates to "stop running ahead and missing what you just passed."

Living for tomorrow is dangerous. First of all, it is not promised to us. We don't know what tomorrow will bring (James 4:14). Second, what we do today sets the stage for tomorrow, so we need to pay attention. We need to revel in our today. It's all we have for now so we don't want to miss the details. Let's store up sweet memories and not allow our minds to wander to places they may not be able to carry us to. Let's wait for the go sign from God before we move on.

I believe Mrs. Shunammite had settled her desire for a child the best way she knew how. She had shifted her focus to the present. And here was Elisha—pulling her back to a place she refused to visit! The same can occur with us when God is ready to do a specific work. The safeguard for us is to *make sure it is God*—not others or ourselves—who decides what our focus is. God is always faithful to perform what He promises. You will see.

Hunger Pangs

- How prone are you to running ahead of God?
- How present are you in life? Does your mind wander a lot? Where is your focus most of the time?
- What types of desires distract you from the present?
- What desires do you constantly wrestle with?
- Which ones have you made peace with in your heart?

Food for Your Soul

Someone once told me this gem of wisdom that has stuck with me through the better part of my life: "Waiting on God does not mean we sit in His lap and look over His shoulder to see if our desire is coming. We should simply settle into the folds of His awesome robe and revel in His presence until He fills us with the things He wants to give us. He should be our entire focus until He chooses to surprise us with additional joys." Beautiful and true, isn't it?

Manifested Expectations

Sure enough, the woman soon became pregnant. And at that time the following year she had a son, just as Elisha had said (2 Kings 4:17).

❦

The Shunammite woman held the child to her breast, lovingly stroking his face as he slept in her arms. So tiny, so beautiful, so real. Though she held him, she still couldn't believe it. Yes, the prophet had told her she would have a child, but her hopes had been dashed so many times before that she had put his prophecy on the back shelf of her heart and not looked back. But now here she was, holding her son in her arms a year later just as Elisha had prophesied. She clung to the babe, enjoying the smell that only infants have. Treasuring the moment, she was reluctant to let him go...so she sat and watched him sleep in her arms. So long awaited, he was her and her husband's joy.

Life had changed dramatically. Their world now revolved around this little gift from heaven. She had pulled back on her many activities to involve herself in the wonderful task of mothering. Her husband was overjoyed, almost beside himself. "It is a miracle!" was all he could say when he gazed on his son. She would never forget the look on his face when she'd told him he was finally going to be a father. She had taken her time, not telling him until she was sure. She hadn't wanted to raise his hopes for nothing. No, that would have been too great a burden to put on a man his age. He had weathered much, and he didn't need to endure anxious waiting followed by intense disappointment. She would spare him that by keeping Elisha's prophecy to herself.

But then she felt her body change. Something was stirring within. At first she thought it was her imagination. Too much wishful thinking. She waited a while longer, wanting to be sure. She had many conversations with herself. *How would it be if I hoped and then found out I wasn't really pregnant? Would I go into a tailspin of depression? Anger? Despondency? Or would I be able to shrug it off and continue serving God with gladness, trusting that He knows what is best for me?* She honestly couldn't answer these questions. She *wanted* to have the right attitude. But the truth of the matter was that she also really wanted a child.

She harbored the news in her heart about possibly being pregnant until she felt as if she would burst. Still she managed to keep it quiet. She prayed a prayer of release, asking God to help her adjust and make life all right no matter which way the verdict landed. She had long ago stopped torturing herself by trying to figure out why she couldn't have a child. She'd stopped searching for sources to blame. Why imagine God's anger if there was nothing she could do about it?

Then she knew. It was true! She felt the child growing inside her body. That's when she stopped trying to figure out what God was up to. The only thing that mattered was that in His divine timing she was with child. And she was more than ready! God's timing was perfect!

The child in her arms took a deep breath and settled deeper into her lap. Her breath caught in a moment of panic. *Am I too happy? If something happens to my son, I don't know what I would do!* Although she had lived so many years without him, now that she was finally a mother she couldn't imagine being anything else. *Amazing! Yes, God is amazing!*

꧁

There have been times in my life when I prayed fervently for something. I believed so diligently that God would hear my prayers and grant my request. And then voila! After what seemed like an eternity of waiting on God, it happened. My request was granted. Suddenly. Unexpectedly. Without warning or notice. When I least expected it. I was frozen in a moment of disbelief. *Is this really happening? Or is this entire experience a figment of my imagination?* I pinched myself. No, it was very real!

God is able to do what He said He would, and He always keeps His promises. We've all heard that. As believers in Christ, we've believed it. That's not what I sometimes question. I find that it is not God's *ability* that I question. "Is He able?" Of course He is! "But *will* He?" That's the rub. And an even bigger question? "Will He do this for *me*?" Ah… And then comes the "What will I have to do to qualify for this blessing I want?" I wonder if my continuous pining for my desire will disqualify me from receiving it. "Do I appear ungrateful or sound like I'm suggesting that what God has already given me isn't enough?" Yes, I can really torture myself and play into the hands of the enemy of my soul by questioning what God does. And yet God remains faithful to His promises to me in spite of my faithlessness. Have you experienced this?

Then comes that sweet moment of deliverance when I hold and possess what I've waited for. I heave a most-satisfied sigh. In that moment I don't know which emotion is strongest—the joy of receiving or the joy of knowing that God indeed was listening and loved me enough to grant my request. The prayer that Jesus prayed as He stood at the tomb of Lazarus plays over and over in my mind: "Father, thank you for hearing me. You always hear me…Lazarus, come out!" (John 11:41-43 NLT). In this case, there was an immediate answer to prayer.

Lazarus was brought back to life and came out of the tomb! But sometimes answers take longer. This is the test we all flinch from. The waiting…But God isn't deterred by what we don't want to experience. He is determined to stretch us and test us with each new opportunity so our character will be strengthened and we can bring Him glory.

When the day of answered prayer comes, people celebrate our blessing and praise God for it with us. What a good feeling! Like a mother who goes through the pain of childbirth, the labor does not compare with the joy of holding what we've been carrying inside for so long. God heard our prayers! He collected every frustrated and disappointed tear we cried in a bottle as he bided His time and waited for the perfect moment to grant us our blessings (Psalm 56:8).

I find it interesting that faith was not really required of the Shunammite woman. She questioned the prophet. She asked him not to raise her hopes in vain. But in spite of this, she gave birth to the promise! God filled the gap between her lack of faith and His ability to perform what she dared not hope for anymore. When God is ready to fulfill His agenda in our lives, all we need to do is show up, do what He asks, and see the salvation of the Lord! Why does He take so long sometimes? He has His reasons. And I, for one, dare not question them. At the end of the day, they aren't important anyway. Why? Because I view with wonder His handiwork in my life and all around me.

If only we could grasp the concept that God is more determined to bless us than we are to receive the blessing. But He won't grant our desires at the expense of not completing the work He has begun in us. I recall when I came to the Lord. I was single, and my entire focus was on finding a husband. Year after year went by and still no husband. Many prayers were prayed. Still nothing. There were times when I tried to make it happen on my own, giving my heart to the wrong men and suffering even greater disappointments than those of being alone. At the time I didn't view those failed relationships as God's protection of my destiny. But over time I finally released my desire to God and got on with the business of living. My focus was moved to other fulfilling avenues, living out my God-given purpose through writing, speaking, singing, and doing all the other things I enjoyed. I found great satisfaction. I was truly happy and content.

Some people found that hard to believe. They questioned me. "Don't you still want a husband?" I would stop to consider this query for a moment before concluding I truly had surrendered this longing. Yes, intellectually somewhere in the back of my mind I did want to experience the love of a man and the miracle of marriage. But it was no longer an urgent matter. On a day when my life was filled with purpose and opportunities to be all I had been created to be, I found there was no space for longing. My life was so full I didn't know where I would put a husband if one arrived! I made peace with my desire, neither running from it nor toward it. I just allowed it to simply be. I came to understand that there was no point in longing for something if it was out of reach. Why make myself miserable? I finally concluded that when it was time for a husband, God would make room for him in my heart and in my life. In the meantime, I was happy to surrender my desire to God and trust Him to deliver it at the right time. After all, if I don't know anything else, I know God always knows best.

Hunger Pangs

- In what ways have you tried to satisfy your desires in the past? What were the results?

- What mindset do you need to adopt to be at peace with your longings?

- What can you turn your focus toward that would fulfill you right now?

- What promises from God's Word can you cling to in the moments that you question His willingness to give you the desires of your heart?

- What past blessings can you call to mind to affirm God's faithfulness for long-awaited blessings?

Food for Your Soul

God knows that "hope deferred makes the heart sick," and that when hope is delivered it is a tree of life (Proverbs 13:12). He is all about being a life giver. He will neither squelch your hopes nor ignore them. He is faithful to remind you that He is a good God and there is hope for your life. In the waiting moments, it is up to you to decide what your posture will be as you wait. Your posture will have everything to do with your ability to be fulfilled as you wait for the promise...as well as your ability to receive it when it arrives. When your faith wanes, remember that God doesn't need your faith, you do. Faith helps you stay in the right place—the place of absolute surrender to His lordship of your life. Faith believes that God will meet you on the other side of your yieldedness. Your trust that God is faithful will help you remain faithful and obedient to His instructions. This is what pleases Him. This is what He rewards in His perfect timing.

PART 3

Where Is Your Heart?

As we wrestle with the issue of fulfillment and what it will take to fulfill us, the big question concerns our heart condition. It affects how we wait—either in a state of angst or rest. As I travel and speak to others across the country and around the world, I hear the same question: *Is the thing I long for from God or me? Perhaps He has not answered because it is merely a selfish request on my part. Is what I long for my selfish desire? Is this why God hasn't allowed me to have it?* But that suggests that if God wanted us to have it, we would have it right away—and this is just not true. As we examine Scripture and the lives of countless people in the Bible, time and time again we see people struggling with delay, with fulfillment deferred.

When people persevere, in the end God blesses them. In some cases we are told they did not receive the promise because their desire was prophetic and for a future time (Hebrews 11:35-40). However these requests were more in the realm of what would affect the kingdom of God at large. But personal desires sometimes took awhile to be fulfilled as well. What was God doing?

In every situation of longings prayed for, I see the unfolding of people's characters to the point where what they longed for took a backseat to their longing for God and His purposes. I see God waiting for their hearts to be in the right place so they could be trusted with His blessing. By the time Joseph made it to the Pharaoh's palace to see his dream fulfilled, he was a surrendered man who would not dare run ahead of God. He graduated from being a young, impetuous boy who blurted out his mind without thinking to a thoughtful man who pondered long before making a decision.

Hannah, who longed for a child more than anything, was moved to the point of giving her first child back to God. She pressed past her selfish longing to care more for the desires of God. In the end she was rewarded far above her initial sacrifice.

The pattern is consistent. God times our blessings in accordance with the state of our hearts. He waits for our hearts to be completely surrendered to Him. In every case, when God became truly first in the lives of the people with longings, He moved. He will not share His glory with another or allow any other gods in our lives to steal our hearts from Him. He knows this would be detrimental to our well-being. And so He waits to be firmly established as Lord and King in our hearts before granting our requests.

The primary question we must ponder is which is more important—the gift or the gift giver. No one can serve two masters. We will love one and hate the other. Will God maintain lordship in our lives if our requests are granted? What or who is our true God? What is more important to us—what we want or God? If God never gives us what we want, will we still love Him? Still praise Him? Still seek to be a blessing to Him in spite of what we think He withheld?

Perhaps what God waits for above all things is for us to gain the right perspective. Where our treasure is, there our hearts are also (Matthew 6:21). Our desires are real and cannot be denied. But God is a greater reality than the things we long for. He is eternal. What we want are temporal desires at best. The financial blessing. The spouse. The professional dreams. They are all things that will not remain. This knowledge puts everything into correct perspective.

When I recognize that as I delight myself in the Lord everything I desire plays into His kingdom agenda, I get a greater picture of the things I long for. I am able to rest because I understand that my desires don't belong to me alone. They belong to God too because they affect His kingdom. From marriage to financial and professional goals, the dreams become pieces of the greater kingdom puzzle that completes the picture of my divine destiny. The more I grasp that God will always bless His program, the more I will seek to be a part of it. To find out how my desires fit into His plans. This is far different than asking God to bless *my* program. As I partner with Him in what He is doing, I get blessed. I am aligned to receive what He wants me to have as He allows me to work with Him on His kingdom agenda.

So often we think way too small. We can't see past our desires. But God can! Hannah was praying for a son, and God needed a prophet for the sake of His kingdom. When Hannah decided to partner with God by giving her son to Him, He blessed her with that son plus five more children! This is the economy of heaven. God places a desire within us. He grooms us to receive it. He fashions us to be responsible owners of the promise for His glory. This should be counted as an honor! For this purpose we are then able to rest in waiting, understanding that our desires are greater than we know because of what they mean to God. And in the light of God's kingdom agenda, timing is everything.

8

When Dreams Die

One day when her child was older, he went out to help his father, who was working with the harvesters. Suddenly he cried out, "My head hurts!"...So the servant took him home, and his mother held him on her lap. But around noontime he died (2 Kings 4:18-20 NLT).

❧

S he felt something was wrong before she had any evidence. It was as if a knife pierced her heart. She stopped in the midst of her chores and straightened from her task, listening for what, she wasn't sure. She made her way to the door to see if a visitor was arriving. And then she saw someone coming over the horizon of the hill where her husband was at work in the fields. It was the time of the harvest, and the sun was high in the sky. Earlier she'd prayed the men had stopped to take shade until the sun hid behind the clouds so they'd have a respite from the heat, lest they get sunstroke. As the outline of the servant became

clearer her heart leapt into her throat. He was carrying something…
no someone—her son. Any other time she would have prepared to
scold the servant for spoiling her child, but the way he was being carried she knew it was out of necessity. She walked toward the servant,
her steps quickening until she was running—already praying that her
child would be all right.

As the servant breathlessly explained, she followed him into the
house. Half hearing the words of the servant, she took her child into
her arms. The man was saying perhaps it was just the heat. The boy had
a headache. A cool towel and some rest should do the trick.

She clung to those thoughts, hoping against hope he was right. She
sat holding her son, her mind racing. Surely it was just a fever from
being in the sun too long. She tried to press past the sense of forebod-
ing she'd had. God wouldn't take something from her that He knew
meant so much—would He? After all, she had waited so long to have
a child. It would be cruel for him to be taken away.

The boy's breathing grew shallow. *Perhaps he is sinking into a deep
sleep. Good. He will surely feel better when he awakens,* she thought.
She tried to calm her beating heart, wondering if its pounding would
awaken him. She prayed under her breath, clinging to him, not daring
to move. And then at noon he took his last breath, and soon his body
grew cold. She held him in disbelief, willing breath to come back into
his body. But it did not come.

Slowly the reality of what had just happened sank in. Still, she felt
strangely peaceful. This couldn't be the end of the matter. She refused
to believe this was the end of such a miraculous story.

Suddenly she stifled the urge to cry or scream. *No, I will not give
in to this. My son was a gift from God, and nothing is lost in Him.* She
would not let go of what she had been given. She sat, caught in a battle
between her mind and her spirit. Her intellect searched for an answer
and all the reasons why this had come to pass. Her spirit remained
silent, oddly calm, as if waiting for something else to occur. She didn't
understand this strange peace she felt in the face of such a heartrend-
ing moment. She wondered at her lack of inclination to give in to

mourning and the persistent thought that there had to be more to her son's life than a sudden, unexpected death so young. But what, she didn't know.

❦

There have been times in my life when I've had the pleasure of laying hold of my desire, only to have it slip through my fingers. I imagine you have too. We wonder why He allows some of the things He allows to occur. Really, now! Why give someone a son after she's waited so long, only to take him away after just a few years? And why grant my desires only to take them away? This makes no earthly sense. What doesn't make sense on earth makes perfect sense in heaven. God's ways are not our ways, nor His thoughts our thoughts (Isaiah 55:8). The path He leads us on to reach our destinies can lead us to valleys and seemingly deep, dark places we don't understand.

This is not a good place to ask why. The question we need to ask is, "What, God?" *What are You up to? What are You trying to show us? What are You trying to accomplish in us? What are You saying?* Why does God break us and then bind us up? Is the breaking really necessary? Truly, we should walk with open hands—gripping nothing tightly but God! Life changes; situations change. Here today, gone tomorrow. Tomorrow is not promised. Nothing is guaranteed except eternal life in Christ for those who believe in Him and make Him their Lord and Savior.

The Word of God does not tell us the Shunammite woman's heart condition, but it is easy to guess. Her son was the long-awaited promise. She was older; her husband was old. They had both given up the hope of ever having a child. Like Sarah and Abraham with Isaac, the birth of their son was a supernatural occurrence. Who could resist spoiling a child and making that child your everything after so many years of denial?

There is the possibility that this son had to be put back in perspective for the Shunammite woman and her husband. This is merely conjecture on my part, but it is food for thought.

Please allow me some creative license to highlight a few more spiritual principles from this particular passage.

At the time of harvest, at the season of fruit having ripened, the son is attacked. Satan specializes in throwing monkey wrenches into our lives at critical points in time when our focus is especially required. We don't want to allow him to deter us or get us off task. We want to stay focused and on track. The Shunammite father seemed to grasp this understanding. He sent the boy home while he stayed in the field. God is calling us to be fruitful. We cannot be distracted.

Next, the boy's head was affected. The head is significant not only of authority but of our thought life....what we believe.

At noon the child dies. Noon is when the sun is at the highest point in the sky. It is when the heat is on in our lives. When we are over-exposed to heat, we run the risk of becoming ill from sunstroke or dehydration. This child was exposed to extreme conditions at a critical time. We too have moments of tremendous pressure in our lives at the most inconvenient of times. We must not grow faint or give in to spiritual dehydration. We must strive to keep our faith intact, to not let it be affected. To not let our thought lives be diverted to things that are not conducive to us remaining focused on what God has assigned us to.

This is the core of our fulfillment—to carry out the work of the Father. Whether that is ministering to someone in the coffee room at work or talking to someone on an elevator and saying something that makes her day and gives her hope. We are all called to be harvesters for the kingdom. This is our life work no matter where we are situated in life. As we diligently set about touching the lives of others, we find our fulfillment growing in leaps and bounds. But the sun will come out. Life will test us. We will find out what we really think about God and His promises toward us—and it will be a matter of eternal life and death. We will either refuse to be distracted or give in to the pain of our circumstance and falter in our walk with God.

In times of loss it is important to remember that God never removes anything from our lives without giving us something greater. A greater revelation of Himself. A repositioning in life. A new opportunity we may not have been open to before. New life. In the midst of God-ordained loss, we will possess His peace that passes all understanding—even if we aren't sure why.

Yes, just because He gives us something today does not mean it will always be with us. Our God is a God of process and progress. He is constantly moving forward and carrying us with Him. Nothing is permanent except Him. Nothing comes to stay except Him. How we respond to loss will help determine the next level of our fulfillment. But we can know that whatever occurs in our lives will work out for the good. With this knowing comes a certainty that no outer circumstances can rob us of the fulfillment God has for us.

Hunger Pangs

- What things in life do you feel you cannot live without?
- In the face of loss, what is your typical response?
- How do you view God when something precious to you is lost?
- What could God be doing in your life at that time?
- How can loss ultimately work out for your good?

Food for Your Soul

In God's economy, loss is never just loss. It is merely a time or place for making room for greater blessings. The apostle Paul said the things he counted as gain, he also counted as loss for Christ. They were distractions. In my own life, the times when I had less were also some of the richest moments I've ever experienced. The bottom line is that God will use loss in our lives for positive benefits. We just need to look for what He is bringing about and trust Him in the process, even when we don't initially understand or see the reason why. Remember, His motives are always for the good.

9

Putting Faith into Action

She carried him up and laid him on the bed of the man of God, then shut the door and left him there. She sent a message to her husband: "Send one of the servants and a donkey so that I can hurry to the man of God and come right back."

"Why go today?" he asked. "It is neither a new moon festival nor a Sabbath."

But she said, "It will be all right" (2 Kings 4:21-23).

S he did not breathe. She did not utter a sound. She touched her boy's cheeks, lingering on their coolness. Still cradling him in her arms, she slowly rose from the chair. Carefully she made her way out of the house to the stairs that led to the roof. None of the servants dared speak a word. The look on her face silenced them. To her no one else existed. She trudged up the stairs that led to the prophet's room. She thought no thoughts; she moved on automatic. Deep within her soul she knew this couldn't be the end of the story. No, it made no sense for her son's life to have such an anticlimactic end.

Surely God would not give her a son only to take him away just like that. He was not a cruel ruler preying on the vulnerabilities of His subjects. No, this situation could not possibly end like this. She looked at her boy. His face was so serene, as if he had settled into a sweet sleep. She chose to believe that. Slowly she lowered him onto the bed of the man of God. She waited. She didn't know what she expected. She stood watching her son, the one who was more precious than life to her, the one not moving, not breathing, not living…

She knew she had to go to the man of God. He was the one who had started this. She had been fine with life the way it was until he came along and stirred up her old longings and dreams, giving her a new sense of hope. He had foretold the boy's birth. And now her son was dead. What could be said? What could be done? Wouldn't the man of God rectify this situation? After all, she had extended only kindness toward him. Surely he would be sympathetic to her plight. He had asked if he could speak to the king on her behalf or to the captain of the army. Now she needed him to be a mediator with the King of kings, the one who commanded the heavens and the earth. She wasn't sure if God heard her prayers, but she was sure God heard Elisha's. Perhaps he would intercede for her. Now more than ever she needed him to take her part as only he could.

She hurried down the stairs, moving past the curious looks of the household staff. Locating her most trustworthy servant, she sent him off to her husband with a message requesting a donkey and a servant to travel with. She readied herself for travel. She was waiting for him when he returned breathlessly to deliver her husband's response. Why did she need to see the man of God today? There was no special religious occasion.

He was right, but she would not tell him the real reason lest he distract her from her mission. It was going to be all right. That's all she knew, though she didn't know how to explain why she felt that way. She couldn't recall the last time she'd seen the man of God. It had been quite some time now. She'd even started using Elisha's room as her child's room, letting him sleep there in Elisha's absence.

Becoming a mother had taken her time and focus away from most of her past activities. Perhaps she had even shifted her priorities without realizing it. Where before she pursued the things of God and benevolence passionately, her energy had turned to her son. Now he was gone, reminding her of the yearning ache she'd once felt at the thought of having a child. She couldn't go back to that place. She could not and would not live like that again. There was no turning back or relinquishing what she knew. The man of God was her hope. He was the deliverer of God's promise. Perhaps he would be the deliverer of new life.

Nothing can be worse than having the very thing you hold dearest snatched from your grasp. To have your greatest desire be realized only to watch it vanish. This one occurrence has the power to devastate even the strongest of faith. Does God dangle carrots and then snatch them away like a ruthless bully? Absolutely not.

What happens when we receive long-awaited desires can reveal a lot about our heart condition. Slowly, imperceptibly it can happen over time. I believe the longer we long for something, the greater its capacity to rule our hearts after we receive it. The Shunammite's husband asks his wife questions that raise a huge issue. He comments that it is not a religious holiday or the Sabbath, so why her need to see the man of God?

What had happened to the husband and wife's relationship with Elisha? He used to be a regular visitor in their home. A visitor they had built on a wing of their home to accommodate. His visits hadn't been limited to any particular religious holiday. He'd been a beloved guest. They'd had a relationship that wasn't tied to religion. In fact, it surpassed it. It may have started because of their curiosity to receive all the prophet knew, but it had grown beyond that as they spent time together.

At some point in time, our relationship with God should move past religious devotion and enter into a passionate union that is sustained, uninterrupted by our longings or the fulfillment of them. And yet we all can fall prey to loving the gift more than the Giver. The gift can become an idol. And God will not share His glory with another person or thing. He knows what we treasure most can consume us.

We're not told when Elisha's visits stopped at the Shunammite's house. When did the man of God no longer grace the room they'd built for him? Was this room now the child's room? Although this is speculation, it is clear that since the birth of this child the dynamics of their relationship with the prophet had changed. And in the heart of this dear woman, that truth clicked and she was able to refocus. She knew she had to go to the source of the promise if there was any possibility of getting her son back. In a sense, she knew she needed to return to basics, to where she was before she received her precious miracle.

There was an even deeper resolve within her. She knew it would be all right. Could it be that she'd decided that one way or the other, she would truly be okay? The King James version translates this verse as the Shunammite woman telling her husband, "It shall be well." Where is her assurance coming from? Paul said that he learned to be content whether abounding or abased. That he could handle being full or empty, rich or poor. He could do all things through Christ. He had experienced being in want and not needing anything. And through it all the one constant in his life was his relationship with Jesus Christ. He was the source of Paul's fulfillment. Nothing external could affect his joy, peace, and fulfillment level (Philippians 4:11-13). This is the height of maturity in God. Being able to stand strong in faith when facing loss and say with confidence, "It is well with my soul."

Hunger Pangs

- What is the one thing that might rock your faith?
- What is the difference between "religion" and "relationship"?
- Describe your relationship with Jesus Christ.

- What conditions have you put on God in the past that affected your ability to be content in the situations you faced?
- What things have threatened to replace God in your heart? How did you keep them in the right perspective?

Food for Your Soul

Time for an "attitude adjustment." These are those hard moments in life that force us back to our initial place in Christ. The temptation for our affections to wander and become embroiled in other things we deem important are ever present. This is a subtle trick of the enemy of our souls to keep us longing for something to the point that it blocks our view of the faithfulness of God or to magnify the gift we've received until it crowds the Giver out of His rightful place in our hearts.

If we're not careful, before we know it we may become "dutiful religious folk" instead of lovers of God engaged in passionate relationship with Him. In moments of intense longing, as well as in those seasons when our desires are fulfilled, we must guard our hearts lest they wander to a place that can allow old feelings of discontent to revisit and consume us. When loving Christ is the central theme of our lives, no matter what occurs or doesn't occur all shall be well.

10

The Right Attitude

She saddled the donkey, and said to her servant, "Urge the animal on; do not slacken the pace for me unless I tell you."...

When the man of God saw her coming, he said to Gehazi his servant, "Look, there is the Shunammite. Run at once to meet her and say to her, 'Is all well with you? Is all well with your husband? Is all well with your child?'"

And she answered, "All is well" (2 Kings 4:24-26).

Her heart was pounding, but she did not allow her fear or her pain to distract her from her mission. She knew what to do. She was going to the deliverer of the promise. Now was not the time to bemoan her fate, to fall into the throes of despair, to wail "Why me?" No, this was not the time to be paralyzed by emotions that would not help the situation. She had to press past her emotions, adjust her attitude, and do what was within her power. The only thing within her scope of ability was to get to the man of God and petition for the life of her child.

She didn't take the time to discuss her decision with family or friends. The opinions of others might be a deterrent at this point. The voices of others might cause her to fear, to question, to bury her hope. The mere thought of that sent a shiver down her spine. Where would a person be without hope? What else did one live for if without hope? Perhaps too much of her hope had been invested in her son. That she could now clearly see. It was time for an attitude adjustment. A shifting of priorities. A dismantling of the idols in her heart to keep only One enthroned—her God. She prayed for forgiveness. But most of all she prayed for her son. Could she go on without him? Yes, she could. But that was not her preference. She was neither angry nor afraid. A strange calm engulfed her as she made her way. She remained focused.

The closer she got to the mountain where she knew she would find Elisha, the more hopeful she became. Still, she wondered why her boy had fallen ill. Against her belief her son had been born. Promised to her at a time when she had decided it no longer mattered if she ever had a child. And now this. Just as she had settled into the fact that her dream had actually come true, it had been shattered in the worst nightmare. She shook herself, as if to wake from a bad dream. And indeed she was awake. Gehazi was bounding toward her.

Stopping a little short of her, Elisha's servant struggled to catch his breath before asking about her welfare. How was she? Her husband? Her child?

She hesitated, debating how to answer the questions. Should she scream the truth or make a faith confession? She chose to call those things that were not as though they were. "All is well," she said simply. Realizing that messages relayed are never as clear as when they are first spoken, she resolved to hold her peace until she stood before the man of God. This was a conversation for him and him alone.

She refused to confess that her son was dead. Some might have said it wasn't right for her not to let her husband know what had occurred. But she didn't want to burden his faith, and she wasn't sure how he would have responded. He might have insisted they follow tradition and bury him immediately. He might have chided her and called her faith foolish. No, she did not want to chance it.

As for friends, they were always quick to think the worst. Though they voiced their opinions in sincerity, they could be sincerely wrong. She didn't want to hear their negativity. She didn't want to be questioned regarding what went wrong or even what she should or shouldn't hope for. Her faith could be affected by their input, and now was not the time to be swayed by outside voices.

She had to hear from God. He was the only One who could do something about her circumstance. This determination had sent her on her way. Ignoring the questions, the rationale about the timing of her visit, she had to go now before it was too late to get back what had been lost. Something inside pushed her on. She held fast to the belief that there was something that yet could be done. God was too faithful to leave her at a time like this. She would do all she could do, and in the end she would stand back and give God room to do what He did best. "Oh, yes," she said under her breath. "It shall be well" (KJV).

On the day the love of my life passed away, I learned one of life's most important lessons—that nothing on earth is eternal save the presence of God in our lives. I was devastated. Did I say "devastated"? If there was a better word to use to describe the despair I felt, I would use it. My world had exploded and fallen down around my ears in little, bitty pieces I could not catch. I wanted to die too. I couldn't imagine life without him.

I hurt physically, emotionally, mentally. Life was unbearable. I winced at every step. The thought of endless tomorrows without him stretching out before me was more than I could bear. I took to my bed. Sleepless nights tortured me, and all the reasons why haunted me. I curled up in a fetal position and failed to function. And yet I had to. I had just gotten a new job working at one of the largest agencies in the advertising world. I was the envy of all my peers. And yet I hurt so much I could barely roll out of bed in the morning. I functioned on automatic. I was like a robot.

Behind the haze of alcohol and Valium, I saw life through a mist. I didn't know Christ. I was new to the ad agency, and all of my friends from school had scattered back to their roots. I wandered alone, trying to navigate through my pain. Looking back, trying to remember my attitude, it seems so long ago, though when I do immerse myself in that moment, the pain is still intense. I had a spirit of resignation. I would never be happy again. This is what I deserved; I was no good. It was my fault he was gone. The voices in my head constantly gave me more reasons to end my existence, to give up on life and love.

Eventually I found Christ, and I was given new hope. But I was nothing like this amazing Shunammite woman at the time. You see, without Christ in our lives what we have is *all* we have. Nothing more. As human beings, we tend to put all our eggs into one basket—the basket that makes us feel good. But woe to us if anything happens to that basket! Perhaps this is why God allows us to lose things in our lives from time to time—to show us where the true source of completion and fulfillment really lie. They cannot come from anything temporal. We can know this intellectually, but the news has to travel to our hearts, to where we really live.

I marvel at the fortitude of this Shunammite woman. Let's look at the facts. She defies every conventional response a human being would make in such a situation. She wants a child for many years. Finally she resigns herself to not having one, though I'm sure she felt a child would ultimately fulfill her. How many of us long for that one thing we believe will make us happy? We all do. Finally, she gets it. Her dream comes true. She heaves a great sigh of relief. And then the unthinkable happens. She loses the one thing she believed would complete her. What a human roller coaster ride of life.

Is fulfillment really that fragile? Or do our souls long for more, for something beyond what we can comprehend naturally?

This Shunammite woman makes a faith declaration: "It shall be well." Good for her! Truly our responses have everything to do with the outcomes. Had I continued to wallow in my pain over the death of my beloved Scotty, I would have lost my job and encountered other serious issues to deal with besides my broken heart. A broken heart and being financially broke would not be a good look or feeling. I had to shore myself up at some point and determine to get on with the business of living. It was the best thing I could do to honor him. I knew that. Did I feel that every moment? No. But I had to press past my emotions, not allowing them to rule my decisions. Attitude is everything. Either we can decide that come what may, all will be well or we can declare that life is over and abdicate completely.

After losing everything that mattered to him, Job said, "Though [God] slay me, yet will I hope in him" (Job 13:15 NIV). Job knew there was more to life. A higher level of fulfillment that could not be taken away from him because it was based on God, not on something temporal. This knowledge gave him the strength to stand in faith with hope for restoration. This wisdom guarded his attitude toward God and kept the door open for dialogue that would lead to restoration and an understanding of a side of God he hadn't been privy to previously. In spite of his wife urging him to curse God and die, he clung to the hope that though he could not understand the reason for his circumstances, if God was still on the throne "all shall be well."

Hunger Pangs

- In what ways are you guilty of putting all your eggs into one basket?
- How much of your current joy and fulfillment depend on having this thing you cling to?
- What would happen if this thing was suddenly shattered or taken away?
- How would your attitude toward life change?
- How can you redirect your focus to something that is not as tenuous?

Food for Your Soul

"Life happens." And indeed it does. But when it does, how we respond has everything to do with how we move forward. I believe that nothing is lost in Christ, and yet we are tested on how we will respond to loss. Recently the airline I was traveling on lost one of my suitcases. I experienced a myriad of emotions. First, I struggled to remember what was in the bag as a way to measure how bad I was going to feel. Did it contain things that were dear to me or things I could live without? After realizing that there was something in that bag I really, really had to have, my angst grew. What if they did not retrieve the bag? This was going to cause me tremendous difficulty! I kept praying. I diligently called the airline every day, refusing to let them off the hook. After seven days of this drama, I took a deep breath and decided I needed to release the bag and its contents from my heart. It was ruling my thoughts and my mood. I decided I would take a break from calling the airport. And, of course, voila! The bag surfaced.

Perhaps God waits for us to release the very thing we are insisting on before He gives it to us. If we believe we can't do without it, it is an idol. If we feel it is imperative to our contentment and fulfillment, it is an idol. Idols will always be shattered at the feet of Jesus. Fair enough. No one or no thing can ever do what He can!

PART 4

Where Is Your Focus?

What are you focused on? What you *have* or what you *don't have*? Are you bound to your desires or to your faith in the One who is able to fulfill your desires? "Where your treasure is, there your heart will be also" (Matthew 6:21). Where you focus is the direction your mind, heart, and soul will go. Your focus affects every choice you make, your frame of mind, and your attitude toward everything and everyone.

God calls us to love Him with all our heart, soul, mind, and strength (Luke 10:27). Yes, He wants our all, our everything. He jealously guards our hearts and minds because He knows a heart and mind divided become gateways for discontent, which robs our lives of the joy, fulfillment, and peace He wants us to know on a consistent basis. He wants us to see kingdom living in its highest form. He wants us to experience righteousness, peace, and joy through the Holy Ghost. This is a life filled with wholeness—God's wholeness.

This wholeness is what makes God exempt from temptation. He desires nothing outside of Himself. All that He desires and requires abides within Him. And He wants us to be like Him—whole and wholly satisfied in Him. We have all we need on any given day because of *His* presence, *His* sufficiency, *His* ability to be our everything. David wrote, "You [LORD] make known to me the path of life; in your presence there is fullness of joy; at your right hand are pleasures forevermore" (Psalm 16:11).

We have access to far more than we can conceive of. It is there for the taking, but only if we focus on the right thing. Like Peter walking on water toward Jesus, life is fine and doable until we look at the instability of what we're depending on. Yes, it is true! We will sink if we look at the visible and take our eyes off the invisible.

I know this sounds crazy, but reality—the eternal reality—exists in the invisible realm. What we see is what passes away. It shifts according to seasons, days, and sometimes even moments. Physical life on earth is not a reality that lasts. We say all the time that things change. And indeed they do. This is why "the seen" cannot be the source of our true fulfillment. We will find ourselves empty and wanting far too often if our present circumstances remain our center. God is the only constant in our world. Everything else is subject to change.

What do we know to be true? The sure Word and promises of God. They are the anchor we hold on to as we focus on the prize of the high calling of Christ Jesus. As we walk toward Him and with Him, life falls into place around us. When the devil grabs me around the ankles, I often say my goal is to drag him across the floor because I refuse to stop moving forward with Jesus! I am focused on what He calls me to do.

I know and understand that the irritations and setbacks in life are mere distractions from what God is trying to achieve in my life. For instance, the tree of the knowledge of good and evil in the Garden of Eden was a distraction from the tree of life. And the serpent used it to deceive Eve. Yes, distraction seems to be an area where Satan does his best work. He waves his hand in our faces, blurring our view of what God has promised and the rich life we already live. He tells us we are naked, diverting us from the provisions God has put into place to provide everything we need. Distractions cause us to question God's motives toward us. Once we get off track, getting lost in despair and hopelessness follows unless we turn back to God.

Focusing on God brings life back into His perspective. It realigns our priorities. Jesus was focused on the Father and completing the assignment He gave to Him. This was why nothing fazed him. Not rejection, betrayal, criticism, or being misunderstood and questioned. He remained focused. He kept saying, "My food is to do the will of him who sent me and to accomplish his work" (John 4:34). "The works that the Father has given me to accomplish, the very works that I am doing, bear witness about me that the Father has sent me" (John 5:36-37). Done. Simple. Nothing was going to stand between Him and where He was heading.

As we focus on "whatever is true, whatever is honorable, whatever is just, whatever is pure, whatever is lovely, whatever is commendable, if there is any excellence, if there is anything worthy of praise," all that would leave us wanting will no longer be able to distract us from the goodness of God and His ability to fill us right where we are (Philippians 4:8). In that we can rest, taking one day at a time. After all, tomorrow will come with its own set of challenges (Matthew 6:34).

11

When Comfort Is Not Enough

"Did I ask you for a son, my lord?" she said. "Didn't I tell you, 'Don't raise my hopes'?"

Elisha said to Gehazi, "Tuck your cloak into your belt, take my staff in your hand and run. Don't greet anyone you meet, and if anyone greets you, do not answer. Lay my staff on the boy's face" (2 Kings 4:28-29 NIV).

Slowly she made her way up the path to Elisha. She was aware of him watching her every step. For a moment she wondered why he didn't come down to meet her, but she decided it really didn't matter. She was more than willing to make her way up the mountain. She took a deep breath and paused to rest for a millisecond before continuing on. It was not an easy climb. She glanced up. He still stood in place observing her. No manner of difficulty would deter her from getting to him.

His eyes were kind and questioning as he gazed at her and waited.

Part of her wanted to burst into tears, but she refused to give in to the temptation. She would not allow her heart to run the show. She was going to walk in faith. This was a matter of life or death. She knew her response to this trial would have a lot to do with the outcome. For the sake of her son, she had to be strong. She would reserve emotion for the end of this story. Finally she reached him.

She could feel her strength draining as she stood in his presence. She had done well to come here, to get this far. Now the reality and impact of what had occurred hit her with blunt force, knocking the wind from her lungs. She crumpled to the ground. Taking hold of his feet, she clung to them, hoping to extract life, strength, and the grace to go on. She had no concept of how long she held on. She felt someone trying to pull her away, so she held on for dear life, refusing to extricate herself from the only source of help she knew. She would not let go until this man of God blessed her. She did not come seeking words of reassurance. She was looking for a miracle.

There was a steadiness in her soul that told her she would not leave wanting. She would not perish. That in spite of what she knew to be fact, everything would be all right. Life would go on. She would not merely exist; she would thrive no matter what transpired.

When Elisha suggested that his servant go to check on the child, she knew that would not be enough. She held Elisha responsible because he was the one who had shaken her out of her malaise of acceptance to reveal that she had merely buried her desire instead of surrendering it. There was a difference. This she knew now. The loss was so real now that her spirit was raw with urgency.

This situation was the prophet's fault. He had instigated her dream's fulfillment, so now he must see it through to completion. If he was able to prophesy life to her barren womb, he could prophesy life back into her dead son. There was no halfway point on this. There needed to be a radical move of God. He had not brought her this far to leave her. Her son's story could not end this way. She would see her request through.

<hr />

How many times have you found yourself poised capriciously on the precipice of what you thought promised true happiness—only to experience the bottom falling out? There is a sense of displacement initially that rattles us to the core. How much of our identity and self-worth we tied up into the acquisition or achievement is revealed at the time of loss. It exposes our hearts like no other occurrence. We can pretend to be gracious when we receive things, but how gracious we really are will be revealed when we lose them.

Once again Job comes to mind. So devout was he in offering sacrifices to cover the sins of his children in case they sinned (Job 1:5). If that doesn't betray how much he loved them and how much they meant to him, I don't know what does. And yet when given the news that they had all been killed, he held fast to God.

In the face of his wife's encouragement to curse God and die, Job refused to do so, understanding that everything he possessed was God's to give and take as He so chose (Job 2:9-10). In the end, Job's fulfillment, peace, and joy could not be in what he had on earth. He had only God in whom to seek solace. Even his friends proved to be hard to bear in the midst of his suffering. And God restored to Job above and beyond what he'd had in family and wealth.

I believe Job was able to persevere, in part, because of his unswerving dedication to God and his recognition that his life belonged to God for Him to do with as He pleased. Job's insistence that God was his sufficiency got him through a period of tremendous loss. It would have been easy for Job to blame others, himself, and even God—especially if he'd followed his friends' lead! They were desperate to find a rationale for his difficulties. But, alas, they could only guess in the presence of a sovereign God who sometimes uses quirky means to groom character into His children and reveal more about Himself.

Everything always comes back down to...or should I say up to... Him. At the end of the day, our fulfillment has everything to do with being where God wants us to be, doing what He wants us to do. Whether we have the things we want or not, being in the center of His will, being caught in the embrace of His divine purpose, leads to a steadiness that cannot be rocked in times of loss, a joy that cannot be quenched no matter what assaults it, a peace that cannot be disturbed no matter how much chaos seems to prevail, and a fulfillment that will not leave us wanting no matter what seems to be missing in our lives.

I believe the Shunammite woman was upset with Elisha because she had settled in her heart the issue of having a child and found other avenues of fulfillment. To be diverted back to the place of initial longing, and then to experience the loss of the child she had become fully invested in as her source of fulfillment, was devastating. What would she do now? She had released all her other sources—or at least made them of lesser priority. Now the void in her life loomed large.

What do you think of the comment, "It is better to have loved and lost than to never have loved at all"? I've always disagreed with it. To have lost something that gives so much joy cannot possibly feel better than not knowing what I was missing! Think about it. When we're feeling fulfilled or content where we are, we don't know what we're missing—so we don't need more than we already have!

Hunger Pangs

- Think about something you haven't always had that is now of great importance to you. What changed after you got it?
- What mindset do you need to have to walk with "open hands"?
- What do you treasure most? Why?
- In what way is what you treasure most associated with your identity and fulfillment?
- What scares you most about losing things or people who are important to you?
- What is robbing you of fulfillment right now?

Food for Your Soul

At the end of the day, it is our expectations of what it will take to fulfill us that can become a barrier to receiving it. The fear of living without love, money, a child, an achievement, etcetera, sets us up to put way too much stock in that person, thing, or situation. This is the ultimate formula for disappointment. Reality seldom surpasses our expectations, which sets us up to crave even more. To attain and lose what we seek may be the kindest favor from God because, in that moment, we discover that life is bigger than the basket we placed all our eggs in and fulfillment is closer than we think if we will only stop directing it to be this or that and simply embrace what God renders in the present moment.

12

Knowing Where Your Confidence Lies

The boy's mother said, "As surely as the Lord lives and you yourself live, I won't go home unless you go with me." So Elisha returned with her (2 Kings 4:30 NLT).

She stifled the urge to scream when the prophet gave his staff to his servant and told him to go and lay it on the face of her son. Though she did not doubt Elisha's authority, she knew this was not what she wanted. No, Elisha must go home with her. She resolved not to return without him.

She had allowed herself to be separated from him before, and the results had been terrible. She was convinced that the distance between them had led to the present tragedy. She had allowed their relationship, their times of fellowship, to drift to a place that opened the door for a spirit of robbery to enter. If they had been where they were before, this situation might not have occurred. Elisha might have revealed that something was wrong. Being out of touch had left her vulnerable, taken by surprise, and stripped of what was most dear to her heart.

No, she would not allow that to happen again. She needed the prophet's presence.

She would not let go of him easily. She would press in. She would place a demand on what he held within. She recognized the power he had—his closeness with God—and this was what she needed more than anything. His presence was required! Nothing else would do. She wouldn't settle for reassurances or placations. He was what she needed. If he came with her and the child did not come back to life, she would know all that could be done had been done and the will of God prevailed. She could live with that. She would yield—but only to God's will.

She knew Elisha had a connection with God, that God granted him the power to change her situation. He was her conduit to God. *How did I lose this in the shuffle of life?* she wondered. What once had been a top priority had taken a backseat to the business of life and the love and care of her young child.

But now she knew she couldn't afford not to be diligent in nurturing this relationship with God's prophet. She would not let him out of her sight. This time it was going to be different. He would come back with her and occupy the place he had before. She had built a room where he used to stay regularly, and then his visits had grown far more infrequent than she cared to note.

Right now her son was in Elisha's room…waiting for him. The prophet must return and reclaim the space. If he couldn't bring her son back to life, perhaps their restored relationship would fill the emptiness of her loss. It had before. *I will not let go this time,* she vowed. He was the only way she knew to get to God directly, so cling she would.

Talk about a determined woman! The Shunammite woman understood the law of proximity. I'm sure the donkey ride to the man of God gave her the opportunity to put things into perspective in her heart. She had time to think about how their relationship had started and what had transpired before and after the birth of her son. As she climbed the mountain to see Elisha, she was reminded of the time she'd climbed up the stairs at her house to see him. That was when he had prophesied that she would have a son. Now she needed a fresh word from him...from God. A sure word. But more than that, she needed an immediate miracle. Her refusal to leave without him wasn't from desperation. Her insistence that he accompany her back to her son was determination to not break their renewed connection. This was a matter of life or death, and she meant business.

There comes a time when we have to decide we mean business with God. When we take hold of the altar and refuse to let go. Jacob took hold of the angel of the Lord and refused to let go (Genesis 32:22-29). He knew there was power in their connection, a power he couldn't afford to live without. Jacob had lived his life scheming and conniving, striving to be blessed for so long that he yearned for a breakthrough. He wanted to be released from the unrest that came from wrestling with his desires. Though they were God-given desires, he had allowed them to consume him. He resorted to ungodly measures to secure them rather than choosing to trust God for them.

Where we place our desires in our hearts, whether they come from God or not, has everything to do with how well we can rest while waiting for them to manifest in our lives. The only way we can rest in God's timing is to remain attached to Him. To walk in constant awareness that He is with us. His presence brings His power, which reassures us that all things are possible in Him. When we are apart from God, we are made more aware of our humanity and limitations. That is when unrest and discontent are birthed. They are borne out of our sense of hopelessness.

But when we choose to revel in our relationship with Christ, we discover a peace that passes all understanding—even when nothing in the natural has changed. We walk in the assurance of His divine purpose and timing. We may wrestle with issues, but at some point the wrestling ends and we choose to cling to the only One who is solid and guaranteed and able to help—Christ Jesus. In the clinging, the things we wrestle with lose their grasp, and we are free to be filled with all that

He is, which is *always* more than enough, more than what we think we need. We are filled with a wonderful sense of wholeness and rest that surpasses our expectations and glorifies God. This is when we discover in the truest sense that we were created for His pleasure, not our own. The mystery is that in bringing pleasure to Him, we find it ourselves.

Hunger Pangs

- What is your relationship with God like?
- In what ways have you allowed distance to separate you?
- What desires have been magnified in the distance between you and God?
- What can you do to reestablish a closer walk with Him?
- Describe your level of longing when you are in the right place with God.

Food for Your Soul

God promises to bless us with good and perfect gifts (James 1:17). Usually the things we long for fall so short of the mark of what He desires for us that He allows us to taste, to touch, to lose, and to release the very things we want and cling to. This is part of the process of maturity—to no longer allow our desires to rule us to the point that they block out the Son. Jesus must shine first and foremost in our hearts, thereby giving us the clarity we need to put all things into His perspective. So that we, like the apostle Paul, can say we have learned, whether abased or abounding, whether full or empty, to be content in all things (Philippians 4:11-13).

13

Awakening

Gehazi went on ahead and laid the staff on the face of the child, but there was no sound or sign of life. Therefore he returned to meet [Elisha] and told him, "The child has not awakened" (2 Kings 4:31).

❧

They walked together in silence. Though a thousand questions swirled in her head, the Shunammite woman did not voice them. She didn't know if the answers would change things, so why ask. *Why did my child die?* Children die every day. Why should she be exempt from the pain that many women suffered? It would be a bit egotistical to think she alone should be privileged to dance between the raindrops of life. What qualified her to be special and free from suffering? She had led a good life. She couldn't accuse God of not blessing her. She couldn't be ungrateful for the seasons she had not experienced major trials or even irritating dilemmas. No, she couldn't really complain.

What does God want from me? she wondered. *Is that the better question? What is He trying to tell me?* But to be perfectly honest, in the midst of her urgency this was not what burned most in her heart. Right now she wanted to see what difference the man of God would make in her situation.

She looked at Elisha. He seemed deep in thought. She didn't want to interrupt, so she prayed silently. Only the sound of the donkey's hooves hitting the path were heard. She noted the beating pattern seemed to echo her heartbeat. Time inched forward, as if God were stretching His arms in the heavens. It seemed as if days had passed, but it was only hours. Then off in the distance she saw Elisha's servant, Gehazi, returning. Her heart beat faster. What news did he bear? Had her son been revived? She spoke softly to herself as she repeated her words to the man of God, "Did I not say, 'O man of God, don't deceive me and get my hopes up like that'?"

She hoped against hope that Gehazi brought good news. The war within her raged as she tried to keep her heart an empty slate so God could write His perfect will upon it. She prayed that His will matched her desire.

As Gehazi drew closer, the Shunammite's heart sank. His countenance told her the news was not good. He stopped in front of them, catching his breath. Everything within her willed him to speak. *Tell me something! Don't just stand there!* She pressed her lips together and waited. Gehazi's gaze shifted from Elisha to her and back to Elisha. "The child has not awakened," he said.

What kind of talk is this? she wondered. *Is my son sleeping? What is wrong with Gehazi? Doesn't he know the difference between sleeping and dead? He's not making any sense. If my boy was only sleeping, I wouldn't have gone to see Elisha!*

She caught her breath. *Can this be what God is after? My reconnection with Elisha?* But now that she was here, what did it mean? And what would be the conclusion of this wake-up call? She glanced at the prophet. Elisha didn't seem to be moved one way or the other by this news.

Elisha drew himself up to his full height, as if determined not to be bowed or deterred by this news. He continued moving forward, passing Gehazi, who turned and followed him.

This quieted the Shunammite's heart. If the man of God wasn't set back by this news, neither would she be. She was going to calmly walk this out. She took a deep breath and urged the donkey forward to keep up. Yes, she and Elisha would both press on and see this through. *God has to be up to something,* she thought.

✒

The Shunammite's ordeal makes me think of Martha looking at Jesus in despair after the death of her brother Lazarus. Through tear-filled eyes, imploring or perhaps even accusing Him, she said, "Lord, if you had been here, my brother would not have died" (John 11:21). That is what we all think when things hit the critical stage in our lives or we feel all is lost. If God were present and cared about us, it would never get to this! This is the great myth in Christendom…that God's love is manifested by exempting us from suffering. Nothing is further from the truth. The Word of God clearly tells us that trials produce experience, which produces character and, ultimately, a hope we will not be ashamed of because we become living proof of the goodness, the faithfulness, and the power of God (James 1:2).

This strange vernacular, using "sleeping" to describe death, is the spiritual language of heaven—seeing through God's eyes. Yes, God views death and loss far differently than our limited view. Sleeping indeed, for nothing is lost eternally in Christ. Delayed, put on hold, suspended perhaps, but never, ever lost. Precious is the "sleep" of His saints because it is a temporary affair. A mere port of transition from temporal to eternal. Not dead in the sense that we tend to view death. For us who dwell in the earthly realm, this is all we can see. We have a limited concept of the great beyond, where the heavens teem with life and the promise of a new earth burgeoning with citizens very much alive after passing from this earth, as prophesied, waiting for Christ's return.

To us, death is very final. God sees it as a new beginning and a continuation of a very exciting journey. That is death in the physical sense. But what about the affairs of life that look as if they are lost? From finance to romance, dreams die a dime a dozen. Where is God in the midst of these times that rob us of our fulfillment?

Just as Jesus stayed away purposely as Lazarus died, I believe God waits for us to relax, release, and worship Him with our trust. He waits for opportunities to glorify Himself but, unfortunately, we limit His work by testing Him in areas that are nearest and dearest to our hearts. We allow our desires to jockey for position with Him. They contend against our pure worship and devotion to Him. Yes, He waits for these things to die in our hearts, our emotions, and our will. But from His perspective, death is a temporary state. The duration or length of our waiting has everything to do with our response and our willingness to release what we grasp so tightly.

Jesus was not disturbed by Martha's accusation that He was at fault for the death of Lazarus. He was more disturbed by the lack of faith her sister, Mary, voiced. He did not expect Martha to have much faith, after all she was a person who focused on keeping busy. She was anxious and troubled about many things, seldom quieting herself to listen to His voice. But Mary should have known better. She knew Him intimately. She sat at His feet. And yet even she was shaken to a point of faithlessness. She too questioned Jesus, "Lord, if you had been here, my brother would not have died" (John 11:32). But that is another story. The point I am making is that Jesus stayed away on purpose and allowed Lazarus to die so that His Father could be glorified and render proof that He had sent His Son. Jesus also addressed the death of Lazarus as sleep. The disciples took Him at His word to such a degree that they decided there was no need to go to see Lazarus since he was only napping. Jesus had to clarify that Lazarus was dead, but He was going to awaken him.

A good illustration of this principle involves a computer. When our computers are "asleep," they are not dead, turned off, or disconnected from power. They are simply reserving power until we are ready to work again. Yes, there is a rest reserved for the children of God. A time to be and cease from doing, so that our strength and our relationship with God can be energized and strengthened.

So now when we look at Elisha, it's small wonder that he was not moved by the news Gehazi delivered. "The child has not awakened," indeed. What an excellent setup and opportunity for God to display once again who He is. In Christ and in the face of loss or death, we choose to keep walking. To move toward Him in expectancy, knowing He is faithful to meet us and fulfill us with His strength and sufficiency.

Hunger Pangs

- What hope has died in your life or made you feel all is lost?
- What promises has God spoken to you concerning this?
- What hopes do you harbor at this time?
- What do you expect from God regarding them?
- What do you think God is doing in the midst of your situation?

Food for Your Soul

A famous ad campaign said, "Why ask why?" How true! "Why" is not a question God answers. Now, ask Him "What?" and get ready for meaty dialogue! When your dreams and longings seem to be the most distant, get excited. God is up to something! Waiting should not rock your contentment level because you know by now that God delights in impossibilities. He rubs His hands together in glee as He anticipates your delight at His display of love, power, and faithfulness. The very thing you think He has forgotten, He has remembered and secured. He remembers more of the details than you do!

Many years ago I became an ardent admirer of the musical abilities of Michael Omartian, the husband of famous author Stormie Omartian. As a new Christian, I was so impressed that a Christian musician and producer could make such incredible music. I thought, *I would love to work with him one day.* This was a dream I tucked in my heart. Years passed...more than 25 to be exact. One day I found myself standing in Michael's recording studio, leaning against his piano, singing as he played. In the midst of recording the song, I burst into tears. God had tapped me on the shoulder and whispered tenderly in my ear, "I remembered." By then I had forgotten, but not God. It was on His list, and in the fullness of time He brought it to pass. How tenderly God guards your dreams and the desires of your heart. Just when you think they're over, He breathes new life into them. You are once again reminded that He alone is your loving God.

14

The Power of Separation

When Elisha came into the house, he saw the child lying
dead on his bed. So he went in and shut the door behind the
two of them and prayed to the LORD (2 Kings 4:32-33).

The Shunammite mother watched Elisha ascend the stairs. She didn't realize until he got to the top that she'd been holding her breath. Part of her wanted to follow him, wanted to see what he would do. Yet another part of her kept her rooted to the spot. She had brought him this far by faith. Now she had to rest in the arms of God and await His decision. This was the tension of knowing God—knowing when to hold on and when to let go. It tested the very foundation of all she believed to be brought to this point.

In the midst of such an unspeakable loss, her faith remained steady. But was it faith…or just foolish hope? She couldn't decipher it for sure. Perhaps what she felt needed no definition. This was not about feelings or even what her eyes presently saw. This was about looking for a miracle. Her intellect and emotions were on hold. Only the outcome mattered—and that was up to God.

She peered up the stairs. Elisha had gone into his room. It felt like an eternity had already passed. She waited. Again she realized she was holding her breath as faintness overtook her. *Should I go up?* she wondered. "No, you shouldn't," an inner voice answered. "Let go." She felt so helpless doing nothing, and yet she knew this was entirely out of her hands. This was the part she hated most. The waiting and not knowing. She stopped her thoughts and strained to hear something… anything. But the air was loudly silent. Nothing. She paced in a circle, just like the myriad of thoughts swirling in her mind. She focused on the pattern she made in the earth beneath her feet. She stopped. *Who was that?* She heard a voice. Then it stopped. She paced. She stopped. She was sure she'd heard it again. She stifled the urge to laugh out loud. How ridiculous! The voice was her own as she subconsciously prayed. Yes, of course! This was the one thing she could do.

Though she wasn't in the room with Elisha and her dear child physically, she could be just a prayer away. She understood that sometimes God needed room to work, and she was willing to give Him that space. Her prayers quieted her spirit as she waited full of hope, full of wondering how God would redeem this situation. She still knew peace deep in her spirit, a peace far beyond her understanding. Everything was going to be fine. She didn't know how; she just knew that it would be. Her expectations had never been based on her own ability. And being totally honest, after considering God's track record she realized that it was only after she released the desires she clung to tightly that God moved and set things aright. Why did it always seem to come to this? Whether it was with her son, her husband, her dreams, whatever. It seemed the end of the matter was always consistent. She was always brought to the maddening moment of having to release the very thing she depended on. Separating it from herself was difficult. *Ah, but then God has room to move!* She stopped and anxiously peered up the stairs again. Still no sounds or signs of life. *What is Elisha doing up there?*

There are those moments in our lives when we wonder what God is doing. We see no movement; we hear nothing. Worse yet, He's not saying anything either. If anything can kill fulfillment, it is the anxiety... the wondering. *Will God come through? Will He really deliver? What if He doesn't?* When the questions come I struggle to still myself. *If God doesn't do this, will He be any less good in my eyes? How much do I trust Him? Enough to open my hands and let go without trying to snatch back the thing I'm longing after?*

I recall wrestling with the intense desire to be married early in my walk with Christ. So deep was the longing that I could find no rest for my aching heart. Everything I did and said was colored by this yearning. It drove my choices and made me settle for some situations and men that were undesirable. Imagine my shock when one of those unsavory men said to me one day, "You know, Michelle, waiting on God is not sitting in His lap and looking over His shoulder to see if what you want is coming. It is *letting go*, not looking for it, just sitting in His lap and enjoying Him." I could have been knocked over by a feather! The source of wisdom was totally unexpected, but what he said was even more shocking. I got the picture. (I'm sure I've shared this principle with you before, but it was worth repeating.) What he said made total sense, but I still didn't know how to separate myself from my desire. The restlessness was interminable. If I could have crawled out of the skin I was in I would have.

Years passed. This comment came back to haunt me time and time again. Waiting on God...looking over His shoulder. One day it hit me. If I were truly sitting in His lap, there was no way I could see over His shoulder. If I were enjoying being in His lap as I should—totally reveling in His embrace, listening to His heartbeat, smelling the aroma of His garments—there would be so many things to distract me from looking over His shoulder I wouldn't even think of it. I would literally have to twist out of a comfortable position and into an uncomfortable one to see around Him. That's when I realized I had never really stopped striving, stopped trying to make it happen, stopped reaching to grasp what I wanted. I couldn't see the forest for the trees. I was too deeply entrenched in what I wanted to enjoy the wonder and power of God and appreciate His nearness.

Though the reality of what we want will always loom in the corners of our eyes, it is what we focus on that will draw us into its center and grab us. If we are absorbed in Christ, nothing else can exercise a hold over us. As I've matured in my walk with God and fallen more deeply in love with Him, I find myself more and more reluctant to release my heart to potential suitors. I am already deeply loved, already full, already filled with all I long for. I'm in a place of great freedom. And thankfully God has helped me be more discerning and less prone to foolish choices. No longer desperate, I am content with God's plan and timing. All is well with my soul. I rest in Him. I wait for Him.

As the years flow by, I am no longer anxiously awaiting a wedding date. Several years have passed with no special man on my horizon, and yet I remain happy, free to enjoy the life God has given me. I no longer ask God when. I don't care! And I'm not talking sour grapes here. I joyfully live in the expectation that marriage is still possible—but only *when God deems best*. I am fine with that. Until that time, I am missing nothing as I fully experience all God is offering me now.

I never thought I would get to this place, but it sure feels good. What happened? I can't really tell you. I'm not sure. All I can say is that somewhere along the way I tired of the tension of wanting and simply let go and gave it to God. I felt the snap of the taut rubber band around my heart give way. What a relief! I didn't realize how much work it was taking to hold on. In the letting go, God shows up and does what He does best. He makes everything better than anticipated.

When God closes a door, He really does open another one. The problem is we don't know when or where, so we have to depend on Him and keep alert. When our insistence on our own dreams stop, a clear path often emerges to greet us and show us the way to our destination. Finally we can see it. Finally we can appreciate it. Finally we recognize God as its source and give Him praise.

Hunger Pangs

- What are you clinging to so tightly that God doesn't have access to it?
- Why are you holding on so tightly?
- In what areas do you struggle to trust God?
- How do you feel when you engage in this struggle?
- What do you fear most about letting go?

Food for Your Soul

Recently I did a body cleanse. I stripped my system of all refined sugar. The first three days were the worst. I kept having visions of Kit Kat bars! But the more I saturated my system with fruits, vegetables, and water, the more the desire for processed sugar dissipated. I no longer wanted it or needed it. I was satisfied with the fare I ate. As a matter of fact, my taste buds came alive! I was able to relish the true flavors of the food. The fruits were sweeter; the vegetables more robust in taste. The sugar overload had sedated my taste buds, causing me to be less appreciative of the good things God offered from the fruit of the land.

Perhaps the same is true when it comes to the things we insist will fulfill us. Can our spirit and our emotions become sedated? Unable to appreciate what God has made available right now? Living for what we might receive tomorrow is a setup for boredom, disappointment, and unrest. As we discipline ourselves to let go of the things that bring conditional happiness, we are released to relish what God provides now.

PART 5

Where Are Your Priorities?

love to tell stories about my dogs. They have taught me so much about love and devotion that I am humbled by it as I ponder how my devotion to God measures up to their love for me. They show me a picture of what true unconditional love looks like.

I know when they want a treat because they sit and look at me so wistfully. But I don't always give them what they want because they've already had their quota and I don't want them to get overweight. It pains me to say no, but I must for their own good. I remind myself that tomorrow I can give them more treats.

In spite of my refusal to grant their immediate desire, my shih tzus continue to follow me around and love me—not because of what I have in my hands but because they are satisfied and happy just being in my presence. They don't care about anything more than that. Oh, I wish I could say that all the time regarding my relationship with God! There are times when I do revel in Him and thoroughly enjoy His presence. It feels so good I wonder why I don't do it more often. But inevitably something distracts me from His embrace, and I am off to the races, getting caught up in the traffic of life, allowing the sights and sounds to carry me away from that sweet place of peace and satisfaction.

If I'm watching my dogs eat dinner and then get up and go into the other room, they stop eating to follow me. Even though they are still hungry, I am more important than any craving they experience. They desire my company and pleasure above all things. They are willing to do what I command because they know I will celebrate their obedience. They don't care if we live in a mansion or a shack as long as they are with me and loved by me. Their top priority is having relationship with me. They know my voice and will follow me above all others. They are not distracted from what is most important to them.

Neither was Jesus. On a hot day he waited to meet a woman at a well. Despite the extreme heat and hunger, He totally focused on this woman's need. When His disciples returned bringing food, Jesus didn't appear to be in need. Talking among themselves, they wondered if He had eaten in their absence. To this, Jesus replied that He had food they knew nothing of. His food was to do the will of His Father (John 4:31-34). Jesus was filled with a sense of purpose that made the desire of His Father's heart His first priority. This was why He had come. This was why He walked in favor with God. God's agenda was His agenda. The peace He possessed at critical times in his life—in the face of unbelief, betrayal, suspicion, and abuse—silenced His enemies and critics alike.

He possessed a peace that passed all understanding. Even being with Him the disciples didn't get it. His joy was such that the world couldn't take it away because it wasn't predicated on circumstances, people, or occurrences. His peace came from His connection with His heavenly Father—the knowledge of who He was in relation to His Father and what His assignment was from His Father. He knew His Father had His back. They were close. Nothing could separate Jesus from His Father's love. He was secure and remained unshaken in the midst of hurt, lack, and chaos. Never in a hurry, He had nothing to prove. He didn't go anywhere or do anything that wasn't what the Father desired. His Father's priorities were His priorities. That was His agenda.

I once heard someone say we need to stop asking God to bless our programs and, instead, ask Him how we can be part of His program.

We know He has a good plan for us! This is how we will achieve the wholeness we desire. This is how we can want for nothing and be free of the distractions our flesh waves in front of us. We need to ask God to help us be driven by His plan and priorities. When His desires become our desires, our hearts will be filled to overflowing.

15

The Art of Surrender

Then he lay upon the child's body, placing his mouth upon the child's mouth, and his eyes upon the child's eyes, and his hands upon the child's hands. And the child's body began to grow warm again! Then the prophet went down and walked back and forth in the house a few times; returning upstairs, he stretched himself again upon the child (2 Kings 4:34-35 TLB).

S he heard him walk back and forth. *What is he doing? Shouldn't he be standing over my son praying fervently?* Again she felt arrested from going up to see what was going on. She waited. She saw Elisha emerge from the room and come down the stairs. He didn't stop to speak to her. It was as if he didn't see her. He passed by and entered the house. She could hear him praying as he walked through each room. Back and forth he went. She stood watching him, joining her prayers with his. She felt as if her faith was being carried by him. She tried valiantly to trust God with all her heart and not lean to her own understanding.

Gehazi too stood silently watching, like a sentry. Elisha went through each room. Prayerfully walking back and forth, then passing her once again without speaking, he made his way back up the stairs and into the room. He shut the door behind him. She leaned forward straining to hear any sound. Nothing. She looked at Gehazi. His calm face betrayed no specific sentiment. She drew strength from that. She took a deep breath and fixed her eyes on the door above. She waited.

***

If the Shunammite woman had been watching Elisha, she might have been even more curious as to what he was doing. My first impression when I read this passage was one of consternation. *What was Elisha doing?* He brooded over the child like I imagine the Holy Spirit brooded over the earth in the beginning.

"And the Spirit of God was hovering over the face of the waters." He spoke and released life into the earthly realm. But there had to be some lifting and separating first. The heavens from the earth, the waters from the earth. New foundations had to be laid for life to be sustained (Genesis 1). Once order was established and everything was in its rightful place, man was created. God breathed into the man and he became a living soul (Genesis 2). Yes, in essence He stretched Himself out over man and exchanged breath for breath. He filled man with Himself. In God, man would live and breathe and have his being. Apart from Him he would do nothing. The very air he breathed came from God!

Surely people in their right minds would worship and be devoted to the One who gave them life and the very air they breathed. Molded by God's hands and filled with His breath, man and woman became an extension of God on the earth. Placed here to watch over all that God created. Formed and assigned to complete God's agenda.

Somewhere along the way, man and woman chose a path of independence. They began planning their own agenda, which got them expelled from the garden—a move by God to protect them from remaining in sin eternally. But before sending them out into the world,

He covered them once more after making a sacrifice—this time with flesh. An act of tender concern despite the fact that the humans had chosen to rip themselves away from Him in an act of selfishness, severing the bond between them in a wanton act of willfulness.

Elisha is in the small upper room with the Shunammite woman's dead child. In the midst of no life, new life is once again dispensed through the exchange of breath. Elisha shares his breath of life with the boy. He aligns himself with him eye to eye, mouth to mouth, hand to hand. Realigning and breathing new life into him.

Perhaps God allows the things we long for to die because something in our desire needs to be renewed, realigned, and restored for greater use by Him. A repositioning, if you will. The way we look at things, the things we confess, and the things we do and touch need to be adjusted because we've gotten off track. God's blessings can easily become a distraction if we don't treat them and handle them in line with God's heart and will.

Submission to God is a day-to-day exercise. Jesus said, "If anyone would come after me, let him deny himself and take up his cross daily and follow me" (Luke 9:23). Paul said, "I appeal to you therefore, brothers, by the mercies of God, to present your bodies as a living sacrifice, holy and acceptable to God" (Romans 12:1). Unfortunately, this popular adage is so true: "The only problem with a living sacrifice [us!] is we keep crawling off the altar!" Today we sing "I surrender all" and "not my will but Thine be done," and the next day we're off to the races, grasping the gifts God has freely given us and promising to get back to Him *after* we've enjoyed and depleted our spoils.

And so death happens. God wants to reclaim our attention and hearts and put all we hold dear in proper perspective again. Understanding this is wholeness…or should I say "spiritual maturity." This is why Jesus could let go of His very life, keeping His eye on a prize for us—an intimate relationship with Him. He laid down His life and had the authority to pick it back up again (John 10:18). He had nothing to prove and everything to gain. He was free to live a surrendered life and be content in all things. Whether staying at someone's home or sleeping in a tent, Jesus was cool. Cool enough to catch His dinner. Cool enough to take small pieces of fish and feed a hungry crowd. The peace He possessed kept Him open to the voice of God and His leading. He always had everything He needed because He stayed in tune with His heavenly Father. And isn't that what we all want?

I encourage you to allow God to reclaim you—your eyes, your mouth, your hands, your body, your heart, your soul. Allow Him to get in your face until you feel His breath. Let it overpower you and fill you. Allow Him to renew you and realign your priorities, your perspectives, your personal agendas. Wrestle with Him if you must, but, like Jacob, refuse to let go until He blesses you.

Elisha got up and walked throughout that house. Not just the child's room, but the entire house. Reclaiming lost territory. Restaking God's claim on that family, that child, that woman. If we don't surrender all to Him, we become like that child—warm but lifeless. Lukewarm—not on fire for the things of God. Existing. Not living as God would have us live or how we would like to live. Forever discontent. Either reaching for things that don't belong to us or comparing ourselves with others, despising their blessings and making ourselves miserable. We need to embrace the fire of God, to let Him consume us. We need to let passion for His will remove all that causes discontent in our lives. There is no more room for wanting when we allow Him to be Lord and Savior in our lives.

In another upper room, the breath of God in the form of a mighty rushing wind filled the house and the disciples. "Tongues as of fire" alighted and touched their lives in a way that changed their vision from the earthly to the eternal. Changed their way of speaking so all could understand. The crowd was amazed as these men, these Galileans, sounded learned, so filled were they with the wisdom and anointing of God (Acts 2). The experience changed the disciples' personal mission statements and what they set their hands and hearts to do. This all took place after a death…the death of Jesus. Once again death brought not only new life but also newness of life that impacted the entire world. Ordinary men accomplished extraordinary things for

God, far beyond their dreams. This is God's desire for us as well. He waits for us to get to the end of ourselves and all we hope for so He can guide us to the beginning of all He has in store for us.

Hunger Pangs

- In what ways have you been brought to the end of yourself?
- What makes you continue to wrestle with your longings?
- What would your response be to the death of your most potent dream? Your closest relationship? Your strongest desire?
- What is your response to God when it looks as if all hope is gone?
- What good can you anticipate coming out of your current situation as you release it to God?

Food for Your Soul

Only when we are willing to die—die to our own agendas and what distracts us from the heart and purposes of God—will we find the fulfillment and contentment we search for. Sometimes our own desires diminish the greatness of what God really wants to do for us and through us. As we surrender all we are and all we have to Him, He broods, hovers, and overtakes us, filling us with His presence. Giving us a new perspective and newness of life that will surpass all our expectations and satisfy us beyond our wildest dreams. "To Him who is able to do exceedingly abundantly above all that we ask or think, according to the power that works in us, to Him be glory" (Ephesians 3:20-21 NKJV). He does indeed satisfy us with good things.

16

The Power of Release

The child sneezed seven times,
and the child opened his eyes (2 Kings 4:35).

A sound startled her. She had been standing in the silence so long…
waiting, listening…hearing nothing but Elisha's footsteps. Now
sound shattered the silence. Soft but no less intrusive. It was a new
sound that called hope onto the scene. She quickly looked at Gehazi,
but he had not moved. As if in a trance, he continued to gaze up the
stairs.

There the sound was again. Gehazi still did not move. She wondered if she should do something…say something. Yet the servant's
lack of movement kept her rooted to the spot as well. What was Gehazi
waiting and watching for? She wished he would tell her what he knew.
After all, Gehazi had been with Elisha for quite some time. Surely he

had witnessed many amazing things. She wished she'd engaged him in conversation long enough to find out some of the prophet's exploits. She knew that those who knew and served God saw many supernatural occurrences. Small wonder Elisha hadn't seemed troubled when she'd relayed the death of her son to him. She could just as well have told him the boy had a cold. She was the one who had added the sense of urgency to the situation, imploring him to come with her.

She strained to hear something besides the prophet's movements. There was the sound again. Definitely not a footstep. More like a sneeze...

A sneeze? Who sneezed? It sounded like a child's sneeze—too light to be that of a grown man. A boy's sneeze? Could it be my son? Her pulse quickened, along with the beating of her heart. Once again there was silence. Then came another sneeze. And another. And another. And another. Each sneeze coming in shorter sequence than the one before.

Then silence again. Why was Gehazi not moving? Not speaking? What did he know? Had he seen this sort of circumstance before? His calm caused her to mimic his actions. A thousand questions swirled through her mind yet she asked none of them. He was waiting...so would she.

~

There is something violent about a sneeze. More so than a cough. It shakes us at the very core. There's a rush. A sudden blast. An expulsion. Yes, an expulsion. In scientific terms, coughs and sneezes are the body's way of ridding itself of toxins and germs that have infiltrated the system. Our bodies are fearfully and wonderfully made by God in such a way that they fight to heal themselves and stay pure of anything that can damage them. If something intrudes, the body tries to slough off the intruder or expel it. Only after continuously being exposed to something will the body choose to absorb it, assimilating it into the system or encasing it with a protective barrier. But the body's initial response is to expel.

This should be our initial response to sin because it is toxic to our lives, whether it be thought, word, or deed. When I ponder what sin is, the definition is simple: anything that separates me from God. Sin creates dis-ease—dis-ease in our hearts, minds, bodies, and souls. Sometimes the things we ingest—mindsets, attitudes, habits, belief systems—separate us from God. He waits for us to ask His help to remove them so intimacy with Him can be restored.

This makes sense. Many couples, no matter how deeply in love with one another they are, don't kiss when one of them has a cold. Why? Because they don't want to contaminate their beloved. They want to protect the one they love from getting sick. Trust me, the healthy one does not want to be infected either! In much the same way, God is repelled by sin because He is so holy...so whole. Two things we are still striving to become.

Elisha stretched himself out on the child and breathed into him. Initially there was a limited response to Elisha's "ministry." The child's body only grew warm. There was no conscious movement or response. He didn't raise his head or even open his eyes. He was merely present, like so many people who hear the Word of God but do not respond with action.

But Elisha was not deterred. He got up and walked throughout the house. I believe he was reclaiming every corner for the sovereignty of God. He then returned to the child and ministered to him again. This time the child sneezed seven times and opened his eyes!

Does God allow things to die in our lives to give birth to something different? Something greater? Something that is healthier for us? I dare say that most of the time there is nothing wrong with our desires. But perhaps our motives for them need to be adjusted. The importance of the desire needs to be realigned.

I think of Joseph, who had a dream that seemed to die a series of deaths before coming to pass. Yet we read about this young man thriving under conditions that would have paralyzed most people. To dream of his family giving him honor, only to be humbled to the greatest degree by being sold into slavery by his brothers—and even worse, being thrown into jail after being wrongly accused! Oh yes, the dream finally came true, but only *after* Joseph and several of his character traits died a thousand deaths.

God was looking for a man not focused on receiving honor but having enough wisdom and compassion to save a nation. The honor was a perk of being inside God's will. Was being honored the desire of Joseph's heart because he'd endured such jealousy from his siblings? I think so. I think it bothered him so much that he implored God to redeem him in their eyes. And God did—but only after he helped Joseph mature and draw closer to Him.

The grace of Joseph's story was the peace he seemed to exhibit through his trials, during which it looked like his dream was impossible. He applied himself to being excellent and content where he was. We don't get much indication of how Joseph dealt with his situation, but we do see his dedication to God in spite of what was happening. He remained resolute about walking in obedience and bringing honor to God. This leads me to believe he harbored hope and trust for God in his heart.

Moses too comes to mind. He wanted to deliver his people, but only after God delivered him of his impetuous, volatile nature and nurtured a very close relationship with him. Soon Moses wouldn't do anything without first seeking instruction from God. The one time he did respond in his flesh after serving God for some time, though Moses' anger was righteous, the consequence he suffered was great. It cost him entering the Promised Land. The fruit of self-control is critical to staying in God's will.

And there's Hannah. While she beseeched God for a child, He waited for her to be willing to release what was dearest to her. Why? Because at first Hannah wanted a son for her own validation. But God wanted Hannah to birth a prophet for His glory and purpose.

When God doesn't bring us out of a situation, it's often because He is allowing time and circumstances to get things out of us that stand in the way of us becoming all He created us to be. While we are pregnant with desire, we find it hard to be comfortable with our circumstances. We labor over what we want, and we long for deliverance.

I see the Shunammite woman's child as being representative of the desires we harbor. He sneezed seven times. Seven is a significant number in the Bible—the number of completion, perfection, and maturation. Could it be that this situation was an indication that priorities had gone askew? Something unhealthy had intruded into the relationship between the Shunammite woman and Elisha and became a hindrance to God being allowed the access He wanted in her life, her heart, and her home through the prophet.

God knows how to get our attention! He will allow our desires to overwhelm us until they die—and everything that was wrong about them dies too. Then, and only then, will He bring them back to life in His time and in His way. He delivers our desires back into our now surrendered arms.

Hunger Pangs

- What do you possibly need to surrender to receive your desire?

- What attitudes and/or habits have made this difficult?

- In what ways might your mindset be unhealthy about the thing you desire most?

- What do you think God may be working in you through the delay?

- What might you need to change about your perspective on achieving your desire?

Food for Your Soul

God knows the plans He has for us. Plans for wholeness, for our welfare (Jeremiah 29:11). He also knows that "hope deferred makes the heart sick, but a desire fulfilled is a tree of life" (Proverbs 13:12). A tree of life. Healthy and whole, bearing fruit that will feed and nourish. Our desires should produce life for others as well as ourselves. When our desires take on a selfish bent, it detracts from what God wants to do with the gift He has given. He loves us so much that He will allow what is dear to us to die so He can restore life and health back to us.

If God was willing to ask His only Son, Jesus Christ, the One dearest to Him, to die so we could receive life, why do we think we can escape sacrificing for the sake of others in the midst of His divine plan? No matter how hopeless or bad a situation appears, we know the end of the story! We can rest in the confidence that God will restore. Everything He gives can never be lost because He hides all things within Himself—safe and whole and full of life. "For in him were all things created, in the heavens and upon the earth, things visible and things invisible…all things have been created through him, and unto him; and he is before all things, and in him all things consist" (Colossians 1:16 ASV).

The child sneezed seven times, and then he opened his eyes. As we get rid of everything that stands between us and God, our eyes too are opened, and we can see God and all that He promises clearly.

17

First Things First

Then [Elisha] summoned Gehazi and said, "Call this Shunammite."
So he called her. And when she came to him, he said, "Pick up
your son." She came and fell at his feet, bowing to the ground.
Then she picked up her son and went out (2 Kings 4:36-37).

"Gehazi!" Elisha's voice shattered the stillness.

Gehazi moved toward the stairs. Abruptly he stopped, turned to look at the Shunammite woman, and then turned back and ascended the stairs.

She wondered if she should follow him, but Elisha hadn't called for her. Strangely enough, she wasn't tempted to follow Gehazi, though part of her strained forward after him. The rest of her felt an overwhelming peace. No, she would stay where she was until she was summoned.

Gehazi made his way up the stairs, turning once again to look at her before disappearing into Elisha's room. He shut the door behind him.

The woman waited. The silence surrounding her was deafening. She stood looking at the door for what seemed an eternity before Gehazi reemerged, beckoned to her, called her to come. She started up the stairs. Her heart was pounding in her ears and her breath was coming in short measures when she reached the top. She wondered if it was because of the excitement she felt or the effort of making her way up the steps. Perhaps both, she decided. She stopped and composed herself at the top of the stairs before entering Elisha's room. She dared not look to the right or to the left. She kept her eyes on the prophet. He was smiling. He stretched out his arm toward his bed where the boy lay and said the most beautiful words she'd ever heard: "Pick up your son."

She had been waiting to hear those words for hours! But now that she had permission, she found she couldn't. Instead, she fell at the feet of the man of God. A rush of praise and worship overwhelmed her. After she emptied herself by expressing her gratitude to God and His prophet, she went to the bed and gathered her son into her arms. She clutched him to her breast and silently left the room. She was speechless...overwhelmed by the goodness of God. She kissed her son and held him, reveling in his warmth. Truly, God was good.

Can't you just imagine how the Shunammite woman felt? Her son was returned to her! What joy! And God is still in the miracle business. From our salvation through His Son to His touches in our daily world, we praise and honor Him for loving us.

Recently I lost one of my favorite pieces of jewelry. After my initial panic, which included feeling sick to my stomach, I decided to quiet myself. Driving myself nuts about it wasn't helping me recover what I'd lost. I kept saying, "Nothing is lost in Christ." I was also able to settle down because I knew the piece had been a gift from God in the first place. Therefore, there was no way He was going to let me lose it! He protects what is His. I directed my focus to waiting on Him to reveal to me where it was. Sure enough, not long after I released it, the thought of where to look came to me. Voila! There it was! As I reclaimed my prize, I made sure I praised God and gave Him the glory. Because of where I found it, I knew only He could have revealed its location to me. I would never have thought to look there.

Isn't that just like God? He majors in the impossible. This is where He does His best work. I often say God likes to show off. He likes to demonstrate what He is capable of. He likes to glorify Himself. What does that mean? *God's glory is a reflection of His presence and His power.* He glorifies Himself in our lives by bringing order and blessing to our circumstances. We then give Him glory by being vessels that reflect His glory. Our lives are the canvases on which He paints His attributes in amazing pictures for others to see.

God allows things to come to a head in our lives before flipping the script with wonderful surprise endings. Picture an exciting movie with twists in the plot that leave us on the edge of our seats. We hold our breath as we wait to see if the hero will triumph. And the hero wouldn't be the hero if other options were possible to save the day. But he or she does save the day...and also makes it look so easy!

The Bible is "His story"—the history of God turning impossibilities into incredible possibilities. From Sarah, well beyond child-bearing years, giving birth to a baby to the parting of the Red Sea, from making Joseph's dreams come true to raising people from the dead, God proved His faithfulness time and time again. And He still does when we teeter on the brink of our faith. As we surrender out of despair, resignation, or even faith and childlike trust, God meets us. He rewards our refusal to give up on Him and highlights the reasons we shouldn't be ashamed of our faith. God is the reason for why and what we believe! He is His Word in the flesh, manifesting all that He promises in His own timing. He recalibrates our hearts and our souls to give Him His due while He helps us put all He gives us into the right perspective.

We were created to worship Him! As we give Him praise and empty ourselves in worship before Him, order is restored in our hearts and our lives. God takes His rightful place on the throne of our hearts. When He is given the room to reign in our lives, all His wonderful attributes shine. In light of His wonders and goodness, all else pales and seems insignificant. He consumes us in His light. We loosen our hold on what we formerly held dear as God reveals all that He is and how He alone can and will fulfill us.

As we choose to lay down what we love most, we set the stage for God to return it to us when we acknowledge that He is our first love. When we anchor our hearts in Him, no loss can take away the joy He freely gives to His own. This joy that is more than happiness or even contentment becomes the strength we need to weather the storms and losses of life. We experience revival and restoration in our hearts and souls. And that brings glory to God as a living testament of His goodness no matter what!

Hunger Pangs

- What seems impossible about your situation or desire?
- How does this set the stage for God to perform a miracle in your life?
- How has your longing affected your joy, your attitude toward life, your strength?
- What needs to be restored in your life?
- What do you need from God right now to grow in your faith?

Food for Your Soul

The world says "It ain't over 'til the fat lady sings." But those of us who walk, not after the flesh but in the Holy Spirit, know it's never over as long as God sits on the throne. We remember that we are created for His pleasure and He delights in showing Himself strong in our lives for His glory and the furtherance of His kingdom. Our personal victories are essential to the purposes of God. For this reason, He perfects everything concerning us and is faithful to complete what He has begun in us.

With these reassurances to stand on, we must also take note of the process of God. Sometimes in the perfecting He does, an entire over-haul is needed. Brokenness is the foundation for strength. That's an odd economy in the realm of the natural world, but not strange in the realm of the spiritual world. With God, sometimes the way up is down, the way forward is back to basics. As we acquire a heavenly mindset and embrace God's kingdom agenda, we let go of worldly perspectives that pressure us to adhere to human timelines and conditions. We learn to walk with open hands, trusting God to remove and replace at will while giving us His peace and joy that is beyond our understanding and explanation—all for His glory.

18

Losing to Gain

Now Elisha had said to the woman whose son he had restored
to life, "Arise and depart with your household, and sojourn
wherever you can, for the Lord has called for a famine, and
it will come upon the land for seven years" (2 Kings 8:1).

She watched him playing in the distance, shaking her head at the
wonders of God and the miracle that had brought her son back
to life. The memory of the greatest test of her faith was still fresh. She
wondered how Elisha was doing. Some time had passed since she had
seen him. It had been so wonderful to have him back in her life on a
regular basis. The conversations between them were richer than ever.
Their bond had deepened after what she'd suffered. They had history…
experiences on a deeper level to share. She had opened her home to
him as she had in the past, and he had come regularly again. The entire

family waited eagerly for Elisha's visits, savoring his words and pondering them until his next visit.

When he was around, everything was so much clearer. His presence seemed to increase her discernment and improve her wisdom for dealing with the issues of everyday life. Life was good, and Elisha was a tremendous blessing. It was sad to think it had taken the death of her son to get their relationship to this amazing level. Perhaps it was true that only tragedy can birth some of the greatest blessings in a person's life. Whatever way it happened, she was grateful.

And then one day Elisha came and told them they needed to move. The Lord had spoken. There would be a famine on the land for seven years. This time the earth and the nation of Israel needed to sneeze. God was going to get the attention of His people. Lack and dying seemed to be the only way to purge the nation of its self-will and waywardness.

She was amazed at her sense of calm as she packed. She wasn't sure where they were going, but she had stronger faith than ever that God would keep and sustain them. She had suffered the greatest loss she could imagine, and God had remained faithful. This seemed small in comparison. She would rise to the occasion and do as He instructed. She also had a new appreciation of her fellowship with Elisha, God's prophet. It was good to have someone in her life who offered clear guidance from heaven itself. She didn't take it for granted.

Not everyone knew of God's intentions, and the famine would hit them unaware. But because of her relationship with Elisha, she had been given this privileged information. God was faithful to keep His word that He would do nothing without first revealing it to His prophets. No, He would not let those who sought Him and His ways be blindsided. He would prepare them and make a way out of "no way" for them. She was open and not fearful. She knew what God was capable of, and in this trust she rested. *Where God leads, I will follow wholeheartedly,* she breathed.

And so she and her family did just that. From time to time she wondered if she would see Elisha again, but in the meantime she embraced the peace of being in the center of God's will.

The twists and turns of life cannot be explained sometimes until long after the fact. What seems a loss may actually be a setup for greater gain. Paul said to live is Christ, to die is gain (Philippians 1:21). This is true not just in the physical sense, but in the spiritual as well. Any time we find ourselves finally able to release what we cling to, room is made for even greater blessings to be manifested in our lives.

For every move forward I've ever made, I had to let go of something. It is impossible to receive if our hands are closed. Yet God often spends so much time prying open our fearful hands! And, yes, I suppose there is a normal fear attached to letting go of our desires. We say, "If I release my desire, will God really give it to me?" or "Perhaps God will decide I don't need it after all, and since I've surrendered it He might not see a need to give it back to me." I've had those thoughts and had to chide myself later.

What do these statements say about our view of God? After all, He is an indulgent God who gives good gifts to His children. He doesn't withhold without excellent reasons. He delights in lavishing us with the desires of our hearts as long as He knows He can trust us with what He gives—that we won't be distracted away from Him and we will continue to walk in obedience to His Word. We can trust Him!

Although my three shih tzus are the cutest dogs on the planet, I insist on their total and immediate obedience. Not because I am a power hungry mommy, but because their obedience can be a matter of life and death for them. One refusal to "come" can put their lives in danger if they dash into the road when a car is coming. I continually practice commands with them so their training is ever fresh in their minds. I insist on their obedience because I love them and want to protect them.

I believe God does the same with us. He wants us to be in close fellowship with Him at all times so we are in tune with Him. So we are open to His voice and consistently obedient. He wants to share secrets with us. Warn us of things to come. Give us instruction that will protect us and save our lives. This is why we need to make sure nothing stands between Him and us. We don't want to run down rabbit trails. Our loving God longs to keep us safe and whole. He knows this is the key to contentment for us—a secure life in Him.

After the death and resurrection of her son, peace filled the life of the Shunammite woman. Perhaps this was the only way God could help her realize her need for a closer relationship with Him and His prophet Elisha. Gone were her excuses of being too busy raising a child. Time with Elisha and hearing God's wisdom was critical to her and her family's well-being. This became crystal clear through her experience. She couldn't afford not to make the time to be with Him.

As we rush about in pursuit of the things we want—perhaps a romantic relationship, a fulfilling career, material acquisitions, a cuter physique—we too must realize God cannot and will not take a backseat to these things. He wants to remain central in our lives. He knows the plans He has for us—and we don't. He has amazing, unbelievable plans that will surpass all our dreams. Built into those plans is a road map, complete with available detours around some of the trials and surprises of life that only God can see from His heavenly perch.

We have no idea what is going on in the realm of the principalities that war against God's plan for us. Satan and his minions are bent on engineering a lack of fulfillment in us and even our very destruction. Their goal is to make us discontent so we question God. This is why intimate fellowship with God is so critical. He will help us navigate around those treacherous traps. He will teach us how to wage war against the devil and be victorious. To that end, He will lovingly do whatever it takes to get us to the place where we will keep our eyes on Him constantly, no matter what we're going through or receiving. And that, my friend, is the greatest gift He can ever give us.

Hunger Pangs

- What things or relationships have caused you to put your relationship with God on a back burner?
- What was the outcome of not being close enough to glean His guidance?

- Compare how life goes when you are in sync with God to when you are not. What are the differences?
- Describe your relationship with God. Why is proximity and obedience to God important for you?
- What do you want most from your relationship with God?

Food for Your Soul

God's ultimate goal is to establish and keep a growing relationship with us that will not be hindered by anything we experience or acquire. This unbroken fellowship is the key to all we desire. We need to keep Him first in our hearts! At times it may seem like God keeps us on a tight leash, but this is ultimately for our own protection. When we consider God's great love for us and all that He has sacrificed for us, we will better understand why He is so protective of His investment. We were expensive. *Tres cher* (very dear), as the French would say. No one is careless with priceless items. When we recognize our value in the eyes of God, we will realize His heart toward us and choose to be faithful just as He is faithful. In this place of deep bonding our deepest desires will be realized. Not only that, we'll enjoy them even more within the arms of our loving God's embrace.

19

Trust and Obey

So the woman arose and did according to the word of the man of God. She went with her household and sojourned in the land of the Philistines seven years. And at the end of the seven years, when the woman returned from the land of the Philistines, she went to appeal to the king for her house and her land (2 Kings 8:2-3).

Time had flown by. It certainly didn't seem like seven years. When Elisha first told her to move to the land of the Philistines, though she had obediently made preparations and set out, she'd wondered what life would be like among these people they had heard so much about. They were not exactly friendly. She had been taught to keep her distance from them, but now God was sending her to live among them. Would God send her to enemy territory? She took a deep breath as their family set out, deciding to trust God for safekeeping.

She had stayed the seven years prescribed by Elisha. She marveled at the whole experience. God had kept her and supplied all of her needs. She had not been found wanting or begging bread. She had not suffered hostility from her neighbors, but lived peacefully and well among them, even making friends.

She had shared her faith and story with many. She was excited by every opportunity to give God the glory for what He had done and use her story to inspire others to seek Him. She was amazed that now she could say she was glad for the entire experience. She was richer, having seen God move in her life firsthand by bringing her son back to life. Some were not as privileged. Why He had trusted her to endure such a trial was beyond her. Certainly He knew how much she could bear far more than she did. She had managed to pass the test and come out wiser and with a stronger faith.

Time had passed, the season had shifted, and she knew she must make the journey back. She thanked God for keeping her as she made her preparations and set out on the road that led back to the familiar place she still called home. A lot had changed over the years. She could see the evidence of the struggle people had endured as she made her way. Not all had fared as well as she. The famine had been severe. Some had been resourceful, some had not.

She heard that the king had taken possession of the lands that had been abandoned. Now she must trust God to return to her what was rightfully hers. "All shall be well," she said to herself. It was not the first time she had uttered this faith confession in the face of extreme loss. She had experienced the power of God to restore; therefore, she did not quake at the prospect of standing before the king. She knew the God who set kings on their thrones and removed them just as easily. He would take her part. He would recover all that she had lost. Of this she was certain. Why? Because He had done it before, so He would do it again. This she knew and believed. This gave her strength for the journey. The anticipated goodness and faithfulness of God was a beckoning arm urging her onward, pointing the way home.

When we obey God there is an assurance that He will meet us on the way to our greatest desires. We are confident we're on the right track because we have been sent by God. "Without faith it is impossible to please [God]" is probably one of the most misunderstood verses in the Bible (Hebrews 11:6). It is not just about believing, it is about the *action* that *faith requires*. Faith without works is dead. Faith requires obedience and a willing response to the instructions of God. This is ultimately what pleases God. He says that He prefers obedience over sacrifice, obedience over repentance. Better we exercise our faith by doing what God says than having to repent and backtrack later. We lose so much when we don't obey God. The consequences remain, reminding us of our actions. Sometimes the damage is irreparable even though God forgives us. The price of disobedience is always high; the rewards of obedience are not always immediately apparent, but inevitably they prove to be worth it both here on earth and in the realm of the everlasting.

This is where close fellowship with God plays such a central part in realizing our dreams and experiencing the ultimate of fulfillment. Our closeness to Him breeds unwavering trust, which in turn births willing and joyful submission to His instructions. Because we know God will meet us on the other side of our obedience, which is exercising our faith, we do what He asks. We have a hope we aren't ashamed of because we have seen God show up time and time again in our lives. Each stretch of our faith becomes easier and easier to weather because God has a track record with us. We realize He is constantly giving us more occasions for Him to actively be at work in our lives. He is faithful indeed!

Lack of fellowship with God stopped the Israelites from entering the Promised Land. It hindered their ability to trust God at a critical point in their journey. When they allowed their fear of God to cause them to opt for Moses being the middleman between them and God, they lost what proximity with God could give them—an abiding knowledge of Him that builds trust. That trust, in turn, is what makes those who know Him able to stretch beyond their limitations and accomplish great things. God "is able to do far more abundantly than all that we ask or think, according to the power [His strength] at work within us" (Ephesians 3:20).

When we know God intimately, we know His character. We know that He cannot lie. He is true to His Word. But above all, we know that He loves us and will remain faithful to perfecting all things concerning us. With this knowledge lodged immovably in our hearts, we have a confidence that will not waver even when we can't see clearly what is happening with our natural eye. Yes, we trust His heart because we know it intimately.

With this deep, abiding knowledge in her heart, the Shunammite woman made her way back home, trusting God would restore everything she'd lost. After all, He had done it before with the life of her son. Getting her home and land back should be easy in comparison. She knew that the hearts of kings were in God's hands. If He could cause the breath of life to reenter a dead child, He could certainly move the heart of a king to favor her request for the return of her home and land!

The palace was in sight. She could feel her heart quicken. She stopped, took a deep breath, and then continued on. "Yes, all shall be well!" she declared.

Hunger Pangs

- What has been the greatest hindrance to your faith?
- How has this affected your obedience to God?
- What were you tempted to do during times when your faith lapsed?
- What were the consequence(s) of your disobedience?
- In what ways has God restored your trust in Him? How did this affect your ability to move forward?

Food for Your Soul

If our hope is placed only in our own abilities, we will never be confident. We are flawed in our humanity, and that will always be illuminated by our inability to keep our promises. The best intentions of men (and women) go awry because we are flawed, imperfect. This reminds me of a game we used to play in grade school. It called for a high level of trust. A person was supposed to fall backward into the arms of a friend—trusting that friend to catch him or her. This was a doubtful venture because the friend could choose to let the person fall. I could never do it because I trusted no human.

But God I can trust. He stands behind His Word and will not let you or me fail or fall. In this confidence we can rest. Even when things look doubtful, we can know that God has our backs. His intentions toward us are *always for good* and not for evil to give us a future and a determined end (Jeremiah 29:11). If we can just remember that the end of the story of our lives is guaranteed, we win because life is not a question of will God do what He has promised but simply a matter of timing—His timing. Like pregnant women who know inevitably they will deliver the babies they carry, we experience a fulfillment that causes us to glow with the knowledge of God's faithfulness. We feel great contentment as we wait upon Him to deliver all that we long for.

20

From Test to Testimony

And while [Gehazi] was telling the king how Elisha had restored the dead to life, behold, the woman whose son he had restored to life appealed to the king for her house and her land...And when the king asked the woman, she told him (2 Kings 8:5-6 ESV).

❧

The Shunammite woman made her way past the outer court, through the inner court, and into the throne room. As she moved past the people milling about, she was reminded of God parting the Red Sea for Moses. Many were waiting to see the king, but she walked through the crowd with ease, as if her arrival had been announced. She was given full entry. She could see the king in the distance. She prayed under her breath as she made her way toward the platform where he sat.

Wait! She stopped for a moment. *Who is that sitting beside the king? He looks familiar.* She moved closer. *Can it be? It is! Gehazi! Elisha's servant.*

He'd seen her and was pointing at her while talking excitedly to the king.

The king looked at her with great interest and beckoned her forward.

What is Gehazi talking to the king about? she wondered. She was excited to see a friendly face in these surroundings where she felt like a fish out of water. She, a mere commoner, was in the presence of royalty. Though she had mingled in great circles before her departure, she had been gone for seven years. She wondered if she would even be remembered. She was pleased that so far her assimilation back into her former standing was going smoothly. Now her curiosity was high. *What is Gehazi telling the king that has him calling me forward with such urgency?*

"This is the lady I was telling you about!" Gehazi said, a big smile on his face.

The king nodded at him and urged the Shunammite woman even closer. She stopped and he leaned forward. "Is it true?" the king asked.

"True, sire? Is what true?" she asked, not having a clue to what he was talking about.

"Is it true that Elisha raised your son from the dead?" the king asked.

"Oh! Yes, sire!" Now she was just as excited as Gehazi. She loved telling her story.

"Tell me! Tell me your story," the king commanded.

That was all the invitation she needed. At times like this she wondered if it was so wrong to be happy that her son had died. At the time the ordeal had felt so awful, but now she was filled with joy that she could tell the story of his being brought back from the dead! How often did a person get to relate such a significant miracle taking place in his or her life? She had a special relationship with God. She had privileged information on how powerful He really was. She had witnessed the miraculous close-up and personal.

This wasn't someone else's story—it was her story. Her story to tell again and again to anyone who would listen. Her story that might change the lives of others. She always felt as if she were unveiling a special gift every time she was given an opportunity to share with an audience what God had done. She never tired of giving her testimony. Her son was a walking miracle. This she never took for granted. Every time she got to repeat what God had done, her faith grew too as she was reminded of God's power and, more importantly, the effect it had on the people she encountered. She was ignited with a great sense of purpose as she realized how this impacted those around her. She was part of extending God's kingdom! This was her reason for being, and she embraced it with everything she had. She felt so alive in this moment!

She took a deep breath and let her story unfold before her captivated audience.

God takes our tests and transforms them into testimonies. I believe the more our tests make us moan, the greater our testimonies will be. No test is fun, but we get the last laugh if we cling to the hand of God and make it through. The important word here is *through*. God is faithful to bring us through and then out. He never skips the process, knowing it is for our good. He is intent on and committed to building character in us. He refuses to short-circuit the process.

I'm reminded of when my grandmother used to process meat and make sausages. She would take the meat and put it into a grinder. The grinder would practically liquefy the meat. Then she would season it and squeeze it into skins that would hold it in the familiar sausage shape. And the sausage was delicious! Because she had seasoned it and added things that would preserve the meat, it would last a lot longer than if she had left it in its raw state.

Such is life. We are broken down and seasoned by our trials in life. The Holy Spirit adds His special brand of preservative to us as we persevere through the various dilemmas that make our lives a sweet-smelling and tasty treat for the Lord to savor. We become delicious because, as we follow His ways, the fruit of the Spirit is borne in us. Through the hard times, we choose whether we will grow bitter or sweet by how we continue on. Hopefully we're choosing the sweet route.

Like a horse being broken so that it can be of service to its rider, we sometimes buck against the training, but we are better for the discipline and far more useful to God. We overcome by the blood of the Lamb and the word of our testimony in Him. Our testimony is the evidence of God being active in our lives. It is the assurance that He is who He says He is. That He is present to champion us through life, and no setback is too difficult for Him. He is greater than the total of anything that challenges us in life. The Word of God is a compilation of testimonies. Those same testimonies drew us to Him and inspired us to believe. When we read the faith hall of fame found in Hebrews 11, we learn about men being raised from the dead, women bearing children from previously barren wombs, and people championing the cause of God. We can link our faith with theirs to believe for the impossible. They all had their stories, and so do we.

What about our stories? With the trials of faith, we have powerful stories to tell. This is the adventure of knowing God. Like an exciting screenplay, every life is a movie being played out for others to see. We never know how many are watching or how our responses to what we are going through will affect people and inspire their faith.

The greatest testimony we can have is how we persevere as we go through times of loss and how we wait for dreams and desires to be realized. The fact that we believe in spite of what is or isn't happening speaks volumes to others and may make a tremendous impact for the kingdom of God.

In the book of Acts we read of people being added to the church daily because of the uncompromising faith of believers who were being tortured. The world searches for people who will stand on principle and not back down in the face of adversity. This is proof to them that what we believe has merit. Everyone is looking for something to believe in, and believers in Jesus who will stand behind what they believe no matter what are beacons of light. People who are searching for meaning believe there has to be something to our faith in God if we are unwilling to walk away even when it costs us everything to stand tall for Christ. This is the power of testimony. Your testimony is not just the words you speak but also the life you live. And that's no small thing.

As the Shunammite woman stood before the king, she knew the power of her story and delivered it. No one could question her truthfulness or cause her to second-guess her experience. She had lived it. The miracle could not be taken away from her. And God wants all of us to have this experience—the power of overcoming the odds in our lives through our faith in Him. Though our visions and dreams may tarry, we need to wait for them. God is faithful to fulfill! We will live to tell of our victory and blessings.

Hunger Pangs

- What is your story, your testimony of the difference knowing Christ has made in a specific circumstance? And in your life?

- How has God shown Himself faithful while you wait for the fulfillment of your dreams?

- What advice would you offer to others in the same circumstances?

- How has God moved in the past that gives you the confidence today that He will come through for you again?

- How can you use your testimony to build faith in Jesus in others?

Food for Your Soul

Two things contribute to our overcoming: the blood of the Lamb and the word of our testimony. The bold confidence we exhibit as we repeat stories of the goodness of God and His faithfulness to us does something to our core. Joy is released in our souls and a sense of awe is generated in others as they consider our testimony and the power of God.

The early church weathered many storms, from ridicule to persecution, for their faith, yet they stood firm, rehearsing all that God had done for them. The gospel spread and the church grew in spite of the many harrowing circumstances. People of the world long to see the evidence of God at work in the lives of believers. People are searching for something to believe in, something greater than themselves, something that can give them peace as they face the difficult and even the impossible in their lives. As believers in Jesus, our testimonies are the evidence they seek. As we walk in the confidence that all things are possible with God, we see His promises come to pass in our lives. They bless us and point countless others to the one true God. This is the greatest testimony of all.

21

Fulfillment Restored

*So the king appointed an official for her, saying, "Restore all
that was hers, together with all the produce of the fields from
the day that she left the land until now" (2 Kings 8:6).*

S he stood back as she ended her dissertation. The king was still
leaning forward in his chair. Everyone in the room looked spell-
bound, marveling at what they'd just heard. Then the hum began as she
basked in the effects of her testimony. Yes, it sounded incredible—and
it was indeed. Her son had died. Now he was alive, standing beside her
healthy and whole. All because the man of God had beseeched God for
her son's life and God had answered. If this wasn't evidence that everyone should want to know this God, she didn't know what was!

The idols that some people around her worshiped had never done
such an extraordinary feat. The Philistines talked about their gods but

not about proven miracles. They made sacrifices and did many things to get their attention but never seemed to know if they had been heard or not. They lived their lives in uncertainty and fear mingled with false hope in idols. Ah, but she knew a God who performed miracles and was moved with compassion for the suffering of His people.

Elisha had made God even more alive to her by the things he told her and the miracle he performed because he walked with God. This was what she had witnessed and reported. She wasn't giving second-hand information. She was speaking what she knew and had experienced! Gehazi had been telling the king about the miracles Elisha had done, but her account was firsthand narrative. And her son was standing there as proof! Though the experience had been terrible at the time, she was thrilled she could share it with the king. The impact of her words was reward enough. Yes, God was alive—and so was her son because of His power. It was a wonderful story and an even greater reality.

After the buzzing settled down, the king looked at one of his officials and gave an order the entire room heard.

Now it was the Shunammite's turn to stand in disbelief. *Did my ears hear correctly? Is the king restoring my land and everything reaped from it for the last seven years?* This was too wonderful to be true, and yet it was. That was exactly what he said. The din in the court rose in the face of this unprecedented instruction. This was royal favor to the highest degree! Everyone wanted to know this God who could turn the heart of a king in such a way.

The Shunammite was speechless in the face of such a tremendous gift. She could feel the worship of God rising within her. She needed to get to a place where she could pour out her praise and thanksgiving to Him for yet another gift above and beyond her expectations. Truly God was good. No—*good* was too small a word to contain what she thought of Him. To Him who is able to do exceedingly—*abundantly above all she could ask or think,* she had to give glory. She would never doubt Him again. He had proven His faithfulness again and again. This was her portion; this was her peace.

When we are in the midst of trials or long-overdue expectations, we wonder if we will ever see the other side of it. But the day comes when God gently leads us out of the trial or delivers our dreams. And we get to tell the story. Not just the basic story, but a far more wonderful story of how He moved past our expectations to do something extraordinary for us. This is the ultimate joy—to be able to announce to the world the reason we believe. "There it is!" we say. "There is the evidence of God's presence in my life!" And we go beyond that to share not just His presence but His power. And not just His power but His willingness to move on our behalf.

Is God interested in the things that cause us concern? The answer is yes. He wants to fulfill our desires. He wants us to experience lives filled with abundance. And not just in the material sense, but emotionally and spiritually as well. Paul shared that he had learned to be content in all things, whether full or empty, abased or abounding, simply because he knew the faithfulness of God to deliver in every circumstance. He no longer wondered *if* God would come through for Him. He knew it was simply a matter of *when*.

In the meantime, there is something to be learned or perfected through Him as we wait for deliverance and fulfillment. When we are convinced of God's faithful character, we walk with grace on and in our lives. No more apprehension, worry, or doubt. No more restlessness. Though we may chafe under a circumstance, we also have His peace that passes all understanding. A resting confidence and fulfillment that comes from trusting the choices God makes for our lives. Of comprehending the height, the depth, the breadth, and length of His love for us (Ephesians 3:17-19). Because of this love, we believe His intentions toward us are always good, always giving us a hope and a determined end as He has promised in His Word. The English Standard version renders Jeremiah 29:11 this way: "For I know the plans I have for you, declares the LORD, plans for wholeness and not for evil, to give you a future and a hope."

Keeping this in mind, we allow God's truth to saturate our understanding and our hearts until we walk freely in the knowledge that what we have or do not have today is what God deemed best. It doesn't cancel out receiving something tomorrow, but for today this is our portion. In this we can be content. We learn to rest in the present and stop wrestling with the future, a future we can do nothing about until we arrive at it. Either we believe that God has gone before us in time and sorted out all the details or we shrivel in an unbelief that kills our sense of contentment.

The story of the Shunammite woman is the epitome when it comes to seeing God at work in the life of someone who didn't have major requests. Her desires were simple enough. Nothing earth shattering. She merely wanted a child, and she wanted her home back. Many long for children, and in today's economy many have suffered the loss of homes as well as work. In this sense, the Shunammite's desires were common, basic. What she received was so much more. Amazing miracles of restoration that opened doors of favor wherever she went.

So often we think way too small. God wants to surpass our desires. He wants to surprise us with joy unspeakable and full of glory. He wants to fill every empty area of our lives with Him first and then His goodness that is manifested in what He puts in our lives or takes away. Yes, even what He takes away are signs of His love and care when they are things He knows will hurt or hinder us.

Those who know God will be strong and do exploits. This the Word of God promises. The operative word being *know*. We need to know our God, love our God, trust our God, and above all things let nothing distract us from Him. Not our doubts, our fears, our longings, or even the things He blesses us with. The consistency of our fellowship with Him will fill the empty spaces in our hearts as we wait upon Him to deliver our heart cries. Closeness to God brings contentment. And that contentment, mingled with godliness, is great gain (1 Timothy 6:5).

Hunger Pangs

- What rocks your contentment level?
- What restores your contentment, even if nothing has changed?
- Where is your trust level with God? What is keeping it at that level?
- What is your relationship with God like?
- In what ways do you feel you need to be closer to Him? What can you do to make this happen?

Food for Your Soul

God wants to do so much more than we ask for, so much more than we anticipate. He delights in surprising us with greater aspects of His goodness than we can ever dream. When we embrace the vastness of His power and the passion of His heart toward us, we are able to wait in confidence for Him to deliver His best. In the meantime, what honors Him most is that we live our lives by trusting Him. Not wavering, we do all that is in our power in the present to please Him and bless others.

God will always honor our faithfulness. In my humble opinion, He throws in extra blessings for those who don't complain but persevere in joyful anticipation. He revels in our trust, a trust built on relationship and a long track record of Him coming through in every instance. When we begin to add those things up, the only thing we can do is rejoice in our present, knowing that tomorrow holds even greater promise.

Though we don't see everything, we know this one thing: We have seen God move before and we anticipate Him doing things in greater measure as He continues to reveal even greater manifestations of His character and heart to us. His blessings make rich and add no sorrow as our characters are being continually strengthened (Proverbs 10:22). They are carefully thought out and timed. As we rest in this knowledge, our sense of contentment grows because we are pregnant with expectation.

Though we might not see the coming blessing, we feel it taking shape. We know that in the fullness of God's time, it will be good... it will be beautiful. He makes all things beautiful in His time. And though we may make plans, the purposes of the Lord will prevail. And let's thank God for that! He knows what is best. He always *does* what is best for us.

Our search for contentment ends when we turn our sights to Him. He becomes our greater peace that brings endless contentment as we rest in His care for us.

Stepping-stones to Fulfillment

- Walking through life with open hands allows God to bless us, use us for His kingdom, and fill our lives with joy.

- The path to contentment is admitting where we are, being clear about where we want to go, and asking God for help.

- What we do with our hunger affects our destiny. Attitude is everything!

- God uses divine discomfort in our lives to encourage us to seek Him and His plan.

- God longs to give us good gifts according to our ability to handle them. He focuses on building our character before expanding our grasp.

- When our hearts praise and honor the Giver more than the gifts, God fulfills our desires.

- God sometimes allows loss to help us understand He is our source of peace, joy, and contentment. How we respond to loss determines our next level of fulfillment.

- Focusing on "whatever is true, whatever is honorable, whatever is just, whatever is pure, whatever is lovely, whatever is commendable, if there is any excellence, if there is anything worthy of praise," keeps us in God's will and brings us happiness.

- Persevering through delays and trials gives us powerful testimonies that glorify God.

- Worshiping God enlarges our view of who He is—our ultimate fulfillment—and puts our desires in the right perspective.

31 Meditations for
Happiness and Contentment

Day 1

The LORD is my shepherd; I shall not want (Psalm 23:1 ESV).

When I consider the list of all the things I want, "I shall not want" seems an impossible thought until I stop to think beyond the external. When I strip away the layers and get to the core of my wanting, I discover my wanting is not just for wanting's sake. No, it's an attempt to fill something that can't truly be filled by any object or person.

"The LORD is my shepherd." We are often compared to sheep in Scripture. Sheep are beautiful but not so smart. They graze along, satisfying their appetites and are often oblivious to danger. A good shepherd leads them to green and safe pastures. He guides them to what is good to eat, to what is best for them. He leads them to a place where their needs are met without putting them in harm's way. He wants them to be full, whole, and healthy. He wants to keep them safe from destruction.

A good shepherd keeps his sheep under strict watch, guiding them and keeping them together. It is in the midst of the shepherd's boundaries that the sheep find true fulfillment, safe and free from trouble. At the end of the day, the sheep are satisfied with what has been supplied. They don't miss what hasn't been given. The Lord is my Shepherd. As we follow where He leads, we will find our desires fulfilled, and we have no need of what He hasn't given us. We're content with today and looking forward to what tomorrow holds.

Dear heavenly Father, help me delight in what You grant this day. I know that tomorrow other pastures await that we will explore together. Help me never to wander outside the boundaries You set and to delight in the safety You provide. In Jesus' name. Amen.

Day 2

The young lions suffer want and hunger; but those who
seek the LORD lack no good thing (Psalm 34:10 ESV).

Want and hunger are two things that can be unmanageable and unending. They can make us question the goodness of God. Yet "every good and perfect gift is from above"—that is His promise to us (James 1:17). In light of that, I choose to accept that I have all I need in this instant. I need no more, no less.

Those who are not spiritually mature have little interest in mastering their appetites and the discipline of self-control, but people who pursue God are groomed for maturity. God is faithful to supply all the needs of those who follow Him. He refuses to withhold what He knows we need, what He knows will be good for us. Although He believes in discipline, like an indulgent parent He also believes in extravagant rewards. If something is good for us, we will have it. End of discussion.

If something is not good for us, well, then, we can forget about it. God is not in the business of doling out gifts He would later regret giving. No, He rejoices over every heavenly surprise He bestows because He knows it is a good thing. He knows that He will reap the glory while we enjoy being blessed. And that is a very wonderful thing.

Dear heavenly Father, let all my want and hunger cease in light of Your goodness. Let me rest in Your choices of what is good and perfect for me. I want to always delight in waiting on You, faithfully expectant of divine treasures from Your hand. In Jesus' name. Amen.

Day 3

I have learned in whatever situation I am
to be content (Philippians 4:11 ESV).

Learning to be content can be a lifelong journey. As we realize that life is not a sprint, that we arrive at no desired destination instantly, we learn to relax, let go, and enjoy the process. Like a seasoned traveler, we take in the scenery of life and appreciate the pictures along the way. After all, we may not pass this way again so we want to drink it in.

There will never be another day like today. Another moment exactly like this to laugh or even weep. Each experience is a benchmark that adds to our character, making us wiser and more interesting, filling us with substance that becomes blessings to others. But we will miss some of these blessings if we aren't fully present. And if we are always straining to see what is up ahead instead of appreciating where we are, we will live in a perpetual state of frustration. Not a good look. It mars the features and distorts the spirit, making us bitter.

So sit back and embrace the process of becoming, seeing it for what it is and drinking in the present. Taste it. Savor it. Memorize its flavor and all you see and experience. Learn to be content. It is not an automatic state of being, but it is evidence of maturity, a maturity that leads to great peace. That is something we cannot buy. It is priceless. Contentment and peace are remarkable bedfellows that sweeten the journey of life and beautify the sights along the way.

Dear heavenly Father, help me rest in the journey and enjoy where I am to the fullest. As I learn valuable lessons that will assist me when I reach my destination, help me find fulfillment in knowing I am exactly where You want me to be. In Jesus' name. Amen.

Day 4

In any and every circumstance, I have learned the secret of facing plenty and hunger, abundance and need. I can do all things through him who strengthens me (Philippians 4:12-13 ESV).

There is a secret to navigating through this life minus emotional drama. It is called knowing where our strength and satisfaction truly lie. I tend not to face hard times well. I rail, I complain, I question what God is up to. I compare myself to people who seem to be doing well even though they don't care about God or seek His agenda.

My unhappiness takes me in a myriad of directions that thoroughly exhausts me and leaves me without answers or satisfaction. I do the dance between extremes in my life until I am brought to the end of myself, which is exactly where I need to be to get to the right place. Eventually I crawl back to the center of God's heart. It is quiet there. And in the peace I find His reassurance that He will never leave me or forsake me. He will not disappoint me. He will cover me and fulfill my longings.

He gives me grace for the day, and I find I have not perished after all. I am standing strong in Him. I can do this—but only with His help. My ego suffers the blow that I am not enough to sustain myself, and when I finally welcome the news I feel such a relief, such sweet peace it defies my understanding.

Dear heavenly Father, forgive me for trying to go on without You again. Now I am back. With You all things are possible. Remind me that it is best to wait on You and lean on Your strength. Help me remember that wisdom when I'm considering fighting my own battles or blaming You for my wounds. Grant me Your strength as I lay down my weapons and take refuge in You. In Jesus' name. Amen.

Day 5

To me, to live is Christ and to die is gain (Philippians 1:21).

How I choose to live and how I choose to die are up to me. I can live a life that makes Christ look attractive to others or I can cause others to wonder at the reasons for my faith.

I realize that in dying to myself I truly live the life that accomplishes what God designed. As long as my flesh is screaming for what it wants, Christ is held at bay. He is a gentleman. He will not insist on His own way. He waits for me to imitate Him and give up my life.

Jesus died in order to gain us. Ah, but are we willing to do the same for Him? That is the question. Do we want what we want so badly we aren't willing to hear His heart and yield to His will even when what He promises is so much better? Surrender leads to death, but that death leads to something far more lasting and eternal. Life and blessings that cannot be taken away. Spiritual fruit, peace, joy, fulfillment, rest. The evidence of God's goodness. His ability to keep and satisfy us.

When we die to self, our goals change. New perspectives come into view. We get a true revelation of what we should be hoping for. We get new life and greater opportunities to live in Christ in ways that encourage others to seek Him too. Isn't it so ironic? Death for life. Those who seek to save their lives lose it, but those who seek to lose their lives and lose themselves in Christ will find the happiness they truly want in abundance (Matthew 16:25).

Dear heavenly Father, I open my hands and say yes to Your will, yes to Your way even if it costs me all that I desire. I realize that it is only in dying to self and living in You that I will discover all I long for and more. In Jesus' name. Amen.

Day 6

God is able to make all grace abound to you, so that
having all sufficiency in all things at all times, you may
abound in every good work (2 Corinthians 9:8 ESV).

God in His indulgence toward us leaves no stone unturned, no empty space, no excuse for us not to live magnificently fulfilling lives. He doesn't say just part of His grace will abound to us…He says *all* of it will! That is a windfall of not just salvation, but also the power to be kept (to rest in Him in difficult times), the power to sustain walking in Him, the power to be obedient to His Word.

As we utilize His grace, we find we have everything we need at all times to deal with whatever comes our way. One time, when Paul was struggling with something he felt he would never master, the Lord told him, "My grace is sufficient for you, for my power is made perfect in weakness" (2 Corinthians 12:9). We don't know how Paul felt at the time about such a simple answer as he dealt with the prospect of never being free of his affliction. We've all been there though. We've all felt that although God promises not to give us more than we can bear, we wish He would use a different yardstick. And yet His Word is true. He gives us everything we need and His will occurs when we utilize what He gives, causing us to abound in every good work. This is the reason it is given in the first place! Not for selfish purposes, but for God's kingdom purposes! As we see and understand God's motives, we align ourselves with them and gain the joy we seek. We become all we were created to be in Him.

Dear heavenly Father, help me recognize Your grace and put it to full use in my life. I want to be who You created me to be, fulfilling my purpose for You. In Jesus' name. Amen.

Day 7

There is great gain in godliness with contentment (1 Timothy 6:6 ESV).

We can't buy peace. This is so true. Something happens when we make peace with God. This is when we discover the source of true wealth on all levels. I find it interesting that God's Word separates riches from wealth on several occasions. God knows material possessions will never satisfy. It is right relationship with Him and the peace that comes from a life well lived in Him that produce a wealth of spirit. Rich relationships with friends and family lead to legacies of amazing experiences that open doors to producing fruit in every area of our lives. That is what results in true contentment at the end of the day.

When we live our lives in a manner that allows God to use us as vessels of blessing that reflect His goodness to others, satisfaction fills our souls. This is an endless well springing up on the inside of us that refreshes us as we walk in ways that please God and inspire people to seek Him. An energy is released that makes us excited about living. It is well with our souls. Wholeness saturates us and is contagious, affecting all those around us with the desire to find the same happiness in Christ. This is what puts pep in our step and light in our eyes. As we commit to walking in obedience and living the lives God designed for us, the pieces fall into place and become the perfect foundation for us to walk in the fullness of all He has prepared for us.

Dear heavenly Father, help me find my peace and fulfillment in only the things that please You. I want to come to the place where my greatest pleasure is bringing pleasure to Your heart. In Jesus' name. Amen.

Day 8

Hope deferred makes the heart sick, but a desire
fulfilled is a tree of life (Proverbs 13:12 ESV).

God knows the effects of disappointment more than we know. He is acquainted with the pain of delay and the even greater grief of denial. He longs for us to come to Him, but time and time again we delay our surrender because of distractions that appear more attractive than His beckoning arms. Still He waits.

We also wait for the fulfillment of His promises and the manifestation of the things we seek Him for. When they are not forthcoming, we question or even rail against Him, depending on the degree of disappointment. We don't realize that in His mind, granting our desire is only a deferred pleasure. It will come in the fullness of His timing. It will come. In the meantime, the waiting is designed to make us fruitful. Our seed of faith grows into a tree laden with good things as we trust in Him and wait in earnest expectation. One seed births a tree, and the tree bears fruit that feeds many. It becomes a tree of life that was watered by tears but is harvested with great joy.

God never disappoints. He is the One who binds up the brokenhearted and restores the soul that faints in weariness. He will fulfill our hopes. This is the economy of God. Our time is never wasted. Neither are our dreams and expectations.

Dear heavenly Father, help me trust You as I wait, knowing You deliver only good things laden with life and blessing in the fullness of Your time. In Jesus' name. Amen.

Day 9

[LORD,] satisfy us in the morning with your steadfast love, that we may rejoice and be glad all our days (Psalm 90:14 ESV).

We're told that breakfast is the most important meal of the day because it sets our bodies on the right track for the rest of the day. It fuels us with energy, regulates our systems, and sets us on our way fully equipped to meet the day's tasks. Breakfast provides our physical food.

But what about spiritual food? That too is needed in the morning to equip us to face the rest of the day. Spending time with God drinking in His goodness, receiving His instructions for the day, and experiencing a healthy portion of His love gets us ready. As He reminds us who we are in Him, how much we matter to Him, and how we can contribute to furthering His kingdom, we are charged with a sense of purpose that empowers us to face the day with strength and joy.

You matter to God. He loves you. He is deeply interested in all that concerns you. How powerful is that! These simple facts will have an amazing impact on your heart and soul. They straighten your back, lift your head, and help you walk in authority and faith. His love fills you with gladness.

Yes, how you start your day has everything to do with how the rest of it will go. As God becomes your daily portion, you are strengthened for the day...and the days to come.

Dear heavenly Father, this day I choose You as my first portion. Fill me with Your love. Fill me with You. Strengthen me for the day. Be my sustenance, my glory, and the lifter of my head. In Jesus' name. Amen.

You give them their food in due season. You open your hand;
you satisfy the desire of every living thing (Psalm 145:15-16 ESV).

What an amazing picture in Psalm 145:15-16. It makes me think of someone holding seeds with his hands open. Many birds flock to the open hand to feast on the wholesome food. As long as they eat, the hand remains open. I believe this is God's invitation to us. "Come! Eat! Enjoy! In fact, take your fill! There is an unlimited supply of what I have to feed to you. My hands are open."

Yes, God's hands are open to me, open to you, open to everyone who seeks Him for sustenance and fulfillment. He has an endless supply and rejoices in satisfying our desires—and the desire of all He created, which includes everything! God created us so He is responsible for our desires. He created those too! He intimately knows our hearts and what they beat for. He knows our cravings. We come from Him, and He knows our makeup. He is not surprised by what we long for and ask for because those desires were literally folded into the fabric of who He created us to be. What we must remember is that our desires come from Him *if* we are delighting in Him. Apart from Him our desires become perverted and selfish, detracting from His plan. As we align with Him and seek His open hands, we find ourselves filled as we feast on the endless supply of good things. He provides above and beyond what we could ever ask or wish for.

Heavenly Father, please help me not be distracted by all the things
the world offers. Remind me to return to feast from Your hands and
rejoice in all that You give. In Jesus' name. Amen.

—⧗⧓—

Delight yourself in the LORD and he will give you
the desires of your heart (Psalm 37:4).

L ove transforms our desires. Consider couples who are deeply in love. The longer they walk together, the more alike they become. Some even begin to look like one another! The deeper in love one is with his or her beloved, the more the person comes to desire what the beloved desires. Preferences and priorities are rearranged. And there is no sense of sacrifice in this. Love simply wants what the other person wants. It wants the beloved to be happy, pleased, blessed! It does not want what the other doesn't want. Simple.

For instance, I now enjoy sushi because a man I loved totally enjoyed it. It was an experience I wanted to share with him. It went from being something that looked disgusting to me, to something I enjoyed, to something I craved. And when we broke up, my taste for sushi remained. If he hadn't been in my life, I would never have been open to trying it. Everything in life is not an acquired taste, but the principle applies.

As we fall more deeply in love with the Lover of our souls, we come to love what He loves and hate what He hates. As our hearts become one with God, so will our desires. Then saying no to the things we once said yes to becomes easy because love is our motivation. Everything is easier when fueled by love and passion! Make love your desire, and everything else will fall into place.

Dear heavenly Father, be my first love! Let my passion for You saturate
and color all my desires. Transform my heart to beat for what Your
heart beats for. Let me find my delight in You. In Jesus' name. Amen.

Day 12

The LORD will guide you continually and satisfy your desire in scorched places and make your bones strong; and you shall be like a watered garden, like a spring of water, whose waters do not fail (Isaiah 58:11 ESV).

The wonderful thing about a shepherd is that he knows where the richest areas of pasture are. In the midst of famine, his sheep don't worry because the shepherd leads them to the best pasture where they can feed until they are full.

A "scorched place," like the one referred to in today's verse, speaks of complete hopelessness and despair. Nothing good remains. It is a place of complete desolation. In this place our bones can grow weak from fear and worry over the future. Our spirits are parched from longing. Here is where God meets us. As our good Shepherd, He guides us to a place where we are able to glean all we need for sustenance on our journey. He satisfies us where we are. He strengthens us because our hope is in Him. We are not weakened. He refreshes us with His Spirit. He brings to our remembrance the things He has spoken and reminds us of His past promises kept. Even though our desires may not be met today, we are content. We do not hunger. We are filled with anticipation, knowing His promises *always* bear fruit. Our God offers restoration and renewal. As we allow ourselves to be led by Him, He brings us into a great place of comfort and peace. A place that holds all we long for—and even more.

Heavenly Father, as I follow after You, lead me to a place of rest and restoration. Fill me from Your reserves. I give You all the glory. In Jesus' name. Amen.

Day 13

*I will satisfy the weary soul, and every languishing
soul I will replenish* (Jeremiah 31:25 ESV).

The exhaustion of wanting can drain the strongest spirit and leave us in a state of disrepair. God knows this. He draws near, bringing good things that promise to renew. Like a spa experience, He saturates us with His Spirit and coaxes us to release everything we cling to. Once we open our weary hands, He pours on the oil, allowing it to bathe us, to reach into the parched places, to coat our doubts and fears with restorative healing.

In the midst of mourning over shattered dreams and time lost, God comes, redeeming the years that cankerworms have eaten and locusts have destroyed. God is the master of restoration. Sorting through the rubble of our lives and the debris of our expectations, He finds hidden treasures that can be used for our good. He then adds to what we have until we have more than enough—a surplus beyond what we started with or even dreamed of acquiring. He alone is able to do this, to do a work so complete that our weariness becomes mere memory.

As we languish, He does not scold or tell us we shouldn't feel the way we feel. He simply feeds us, knowing the journey ahead will not be abandoned once we have been refreshed and strengthened to continue. So He sets His sights on equipping us to continue…continue on the path that He has laid out before us. He is taking us somewhere good, of this we can be sure.

*Dear heavenly Father, feed me, renew me, restore me. I wait on You—
and only You—to be my strength. In Jesus' name. Amen.*

Day 14

Blessed is the one you choose and bring near, to dwell in your courts! We shall be satisfied with the goodness of your house, the holiness of your temple! (Psalm 65:4 ESV).

People who stand afar off from God are more likely to experience hunger than those who enter into His presence. I can vouch for this. I recall my life before I walked with God. Though I had much materially, I always wondered if there wasn't more to life than what I was experiencing. There's an interesting thing about lack. As long as we are experiencing it, we have something to blame for our discontent. But what happens when there is no apparent lack and we still feel empty? This is where I found myself. It was excruciating because there was no rhyme or apparent reason for my unrest and dissatisfaction. Ah, but then I wandered past all my acquisitions and found God. When I embraced Him in all His fullness and started spending time in His house, I was filled to overflowing with a great sense of completion. There is goodness in His house! I feasted on His Word and found purification, life, and joy. I fellowshipped with His people and found comfort and encouragement. God became my respite in the midst of my longings. Suddenly all I had was enough—actually more than enough.

Dear heavenly Father, as I choose to spend time with You in Your house among Your people, please fill me with all You are. I know I will not be left wanting in You. In Jesus' name. Amen.

Day 15

The fear of the LORD leads to life, and whoever
has it rests satisfied (Proverbs 19:23 ESV).

The acknowledgment of the awesomeness of God is not just about shivering and shaking in our boots. It is realizing His greatness and power at work on our behalf. It is knowing that the One who has our back and our best interest at heart also has the power to deliver what He wants to in our lives. It is the realization that God is God and we are not. This should be a relief! We are not hindered by our own finiteness, our own humanity with all its limitations. No, our lives are in the hands of the One who has all power in His hands!

God makes things happen—and how! We can rest in that fact. We don't have to wonder if He can deliver or will. We know He can and does. We don't have to wonder if circumstances will circumvent His plans for our lives. If God is doing it, nothing can hinder His work! He is able to watch over His work and perform in amazing ways that confound even the wise.

While we wait on Him to act, He also dispenses His grace to keep us, fill us, and empower us to hold on a little while longer. Oh yes, God is great and greatly to be praised! What He says He will do He will do—no ifs, ands, or buts. He stands behind His Word to perform it and then perfects everything concerning us. He becomes our expectation as we trust Him completely and resist the urge to lean on our own understanding. His ways are not our ways, rest assured. He will come through for us. This certainty is our comfort.

Dear heavenly Father, my eyes are on You. I rest, I wait, I trust. Meet me here. In Jesus' name. Amen.

Day 16

Endurance produces character, and character produces hope, and hope does not put us to shame, because God's love has been poured into our hearts through the Holy Spirit who has been given to us (Romans 5:4-5 ESV).

There is something to be gained in waiting. Perhaps we can't hold it in our hands, but we can definitely hold it in our hearts, where things last longer. The discomfort of wondering and waiting gives way to something stronger and of greater weight. An internal intangible that manifests in the way we live our lives, the choices we make, and the ultimate outcome of the situation. What is it? *Endurance.*

Endurance is not for the faint of heart, but neither is waiting. As we choose how we wait—whether to trust God and rest or to question Him and fret—our posture affects how we move forward. We can grow bitter or grow better—it's up to us. To choose the latter means we fortify our spirits in the knowledge of who God says He is. As that unfolds and manifests, our views are solidified on God, our desires, how things fit together, who we are through all of this at the end of the day, and the foundation of what we believe based on what we just experienced.

If we stick with God, we will not be disappointed. And we will hold the proof of why we shouldn't be. And the next time a question is raised we will know the answer sooner because of what God has already shown us. This is wonderful and true. No pain, no gain, as they say. And that's what makes the whole experience even more fulfilling. Happy endings have a way of doing that. Suddenly when everything falls into place, all it took to get there is worth it.

Dear heavenly Father, complete what You have begun in me. In Jesus' name. Amen.

Day 17

Blessed are those who hunger and thirst for righteousness,
for they shall be satisfied (Matthew 5:6 ESV).

Perhaps it's not so much "wanting" that gets us into trouble. No, it's more *what* we want. When we want the wrong things, fulfillment is hard to come by. The very thing we want continues to elude us. I've noticed on several occasions that the moment I went looking for something specific, I couldn't find it—only later to find it after the item was no longer on my want list or even important to me. And usually I find whatever it was in abundance everywhere!

Perhaps my wanting blinded me to what I really needed to be wanting. God's Word tells us what to desire, along with providing the promise that we will not be left wanting if we seek what God wants for us. As a matter of fact, the Bible is very specific. It notes that if we hunger and thirst for righteousness, being totally committed to the desire, we will be filled, satisfied, and happy. If our first focus of want is to desire God, to be right with Him, to be friends with Him, to be in right relationship with Him, we will be satisfied.

But if we get distracted by wanting all manner of other things before seeking God, we will continue wanting. We will be hungry, we will be thirsty, we will be insatiable, we will be overwhelmed with a sense of a vacuum in the core of our being. This vast emptiness will haunt us as we wrestle with how to fill it. "What will it take to be happy?" we ask. The answer seems too simple. Surely we need more than an intangible relationship with God. But we don't. In Him is total fulfillment and happiness and contentment.

Dear heavenly Father, You are the obvious missing link in my search
for fulfillment. Restore me completely to You. In Jesus' name. Amen.

Day 18

Indeed, none who wait for you [LORD,]
shall be put to shame (Psalm 25:3 ESV).

Life in the Spirit of God is so contrary to the rules of the world that we feel almost ridiculous at times when we choose to err on the side of faith instead of resorting to the hustle and bustle that the secular world thrives on. "We've got to make 'it' happen!" they say. "We have to do whatever it takes to make our dreams come true."

But this goes against the very grain of what the Holy Spirit says: Wait on God. "What?" we say. "How can we wait on God? We've got to *do* something!" And yet God never asks us to do anything to make something happen. He asks us to simply "be" in Him. Be still, be holy, be mature…these all speak to holding a specific posture rather than being busy creating a mess for ourselves.

When God creates in the midst of our stillness, it is always beautiful and surpasses our expectations. We will have bragging rights, but not on our own ability. No, it comes to pass solely on the power of God and His power at work in us, through us, and around us. Yes, the results will all come back to God, glorifying Him. And as we praise Him for bringing it to pass, we're deflected from focusing on our own short-comings and inability to "make things happen," as the world would say. We know the One who speaks a word and it happens! He says "Let it be," and it is so. That's the kind of stuff I'm talking about! God is truly amazing, and He delights in amazing us as we stand still and see His work in every situation in our lives—even those we thought hopeless.

Dear heavenly Father, I struggle with this concept of stillness. Speak to the troubled waters of my soul and bid me to be still in You. Help me trust You as I wait for You to complete all things concerning me. In Jesus' name. Amen.

You shall no more be termed Forsaken, and your land shall no more be termed Desolate, but you shall be called My Delight Is in Her, and your land Married; for the LORD delights in you, and your land shall be married (Isaiah 62:4 ESV).

As we wait for the fulfillment of our desires, we need to remember that our desires are greater than just a personal issue. The reputation of God is at stake! People are watching and evaluating God based on what they see occurring in our lives. Moses reminded God of this on the way to the Promised Land when God was furious with the Israelites for forsaking Him and chasing idols. And God honored His covenant with His people for generations, regardless of their faithlessness simply because His name was and is at stake.

"Forsaken" and "Desolate" are not names He desires us to have. If we are delighting in Him, then we are His delight and His favor will be manifested in our lives. Whether it is the joy we convey despite the fact our circumstances aren't ideal or because amazing miracles have occurred, others are taking note that we are walking with God and He is honoring His covenant with us.

Marriage is an unconditional covenant. We are called the bride of Christ. Like a faithful groom, He cares for His bride—us—and shows Himself strong in our lives as we remember His promises and walk in expectancy, not giving in to feelings of being alone or forsaken. God arises and always shows Himself faithful.

Dear heavenly Father, as I remind myself that I am not alone, continue Your faithfulness toward me so people around me will see Your goodness at work and desire to know You. In Jesus' name. Amen.

I wait for the LORD, my soul waits,
and in his word I hope (Psalm 130:5 ESV).

What are you waiting for? Where are your eyes focused? What is the source of your expectation? "I wait for the LORD." There have been so many times in life that people, in their humanity, have disappointed me. Perhaps I expected too much. Or I used myself as a ruler, failing to consider the times I also let others down. Not intentionally, sure, but nevertheless I did. The bottom line is that people will fail us. And we will fail others. But God never fails! If He promised to do it, He will do it.

Here is where we have to walk circumspectly. Are we asking God to fulfill our wishes? Or are we waiting for God to fulfill His wishes for us? If I ask in the will of the Father, He is faithful to answer and grant me my request. But if I simply decide to dictate to God what I want without consulting to see if He agrees, I set myself up for great disappointment. It is far better to become part of God's agenda versus demanding that God become part of ours. We need to wait on Him, not on what we want. Trusting in His Word and His promises, we can possess a peace that passes all understanding, knowing that in the fullness of time the things we wait for will indeed be manifest. Because of the perfect timing of God, they will be blessings that make rich and add no sorrow. It is a matter of trust. Where our attention is focused will make the wait a dirge or a delight. We who hope in God and delight in Him will find delight.

Dear heavenly Father, as I turn my eyes to You, let me find my peace in You. Free from the distractions of things I seek. In Jesus' name. Amen.

Day 21

God is not a God of confusion but of peace (1 Corinthians 14:33 ESV).

If there is angst in our waiting, we need to turn to God and seek Him again, to ask Him which area of our desire has been misdirected. An old adage goes like this:

> When the situation is wrong and you are wrong, God says no. When the situation is right and you are wrong, God says grow. When you are right and the situation is wrong, God says slow. When you are right and the situation is right, God says go.

This bit of wisdom has helped me so many times as I struggle with my desires. If I give in to frustration and question God, I find myself in confusion. Is God playing a trick on me? Is He withholding my desire just because He can? Do I want it too badly? Did He say I could have it—or was it just my imagination because I wanted it so badly? Is my faith not strong enough? Is that why I'm not getting what I yearn for? On and on the questions assault me, bringing me to a place of great unrest. The joy in the things I already possess disintegrates, and I find I'm not happy with anything. This is the first clue that something is wrong. God does not create unrest. He has reserved rest for us if we'll only enter in by letting go of the things we insist on.

Friend, pursue God's peace with all that is within you. Don't let the voices without or within distract you from His voice, His comfort, His assurances, His Word. He provides unwavering strength for your journey. As you remain married to Him versus being married to what you want, you will be overwhelmed by His peace.

Dear heavenly Father, let Your peace abide with me as I abide in You. In Jesus' name. Amen.

Day 22

The Lord waits to be gracious to you, and therefore he exalts himself to show mercy to you (Isaiah 30:18 ESV).

Wow! The Lord is waiting to reveal Himself and His grace to us! That is huge. It tells of longing on the part of God to do good things for us, to bestow His benevolence on us, to extend to us all the things He has planned for us. But *He waits.* What is He waiting for? Perhaps for us to get into the right position mentally, physically, emotionally, and spiritually so we can more fully receive the things He so passionately wants to give.

So often we feel that we are the only ones endlessly waiting for things to come to pass in our lives. We wonder if God truly understands and relates to the pain of waiting, to the grief of longing for something, to the wondering if we will ever receive our heart's desire. As we fidget and maneuver our hearts and emotions to find a comfortable place in the midst of the waiting, we once again ponder how God feels. Has He ever had to wait for anything? The answer is yes! He waits for us to be reconciled to Him. He waits for us to make Him our preference over all things. He waits for us to love Him the way He loves us. He waits for us to walk in obedience to Him.

Oh, my friend, God is well acquainted with waiting! He waits for us to become all He created us to be and acquire. He is our portion and reward, and we are His joy. He constantly cares about our welfare. He waits to exalt Himself and reveal His goodness to us. He wants to be our greatest joy so that our joy can never be taken away.

Dear heavenly Father, I pray that I am worth the wait. In Jesus' name. Amen.

Day 23

They who wait for the LORD shall renew their strength; they shall mount up with wings like eagles; they shall run and not be weary; they shall walk and not faint (Isaiah 40:31 ESV).

Perhaps we rebel against waiting for God because it sounds so helpless, so…out of control, inactive, passive. We are not people who take very well to just allowing things to happen. We are a "make it happen" society. Anything less is simply not admirable. However, this attitude is not necessarily true. There is an active aspect of waiting.

A person who waits on another, as in serving another, chooses to await instructions or requests and then carry them out. In the doing, there is the reward of knowing the pleasure of the one being served as we deliver what was asked for. I waited on tables when I was in college and was paid handsome tips because of my good service. When we wait on God, as in when we serve God, we become energized by the aspect of pleasing Him. Whenever we are active, energy is released. And energy releases more energy. Waiting on God doesn't have to be a lethargic exercise. Part of being happy where we are is making the most of where we are. Setting our hands to do what we can do for the Lord will always open doors for more opportunities and blessings. Waiting is not the issue. How we wait is.

Dear heavenly Father, please forgive me for my stagnancy. Forgive me for digging in my heels, refusing to serve You until my needs are met. Help me find the joy in serving You so my zest for life is restored. Renew and revive me as I willingly follow Your requests. In Jesus' name. Amen.

Day 24

*It is good to wait quietly for the salvation
of the LORD* (Lamentations 3:26).

Another aspect of waiting that often gets us into trouble is the things we say. We're like the petulant little girl who, when told to sit down, does so but announces she is still standing up inside. We too tell the world that while we may be sitting, that is not our posture inwardly. Sometimes we go through the motions of waiting on God, but all the while we complain about the wait. Or we're comparing ourselves to others who seem to be faring better with getting what they want from God. Or we're questioning, sometimes railing at, God and His time schedule.

Again I think of my waitressing time. I wanted to do my best for the customers who were patient. The ones who were not kind, who were impatient vocally, caused me to stall. I made them suffer in subtle ways. After all, I was the one who had access to what they wanted. The nastier they were, the longer I made them wait. Have you heard the warning that we should never insult someone who has the ability to spit in our food? (No, I never stooped to anything like that!) Although God is not spiteful, it is good to wait on Him quietly and patiently. Cease from clamoring and complaining. Stop questioning and grumbling. Complaining begets more complaining. It is good to wait with anticipation instead of impatience because God is good. Our silent attention is our acknowledgment of that goodness as well as our trust in Him. Silence signals gratefulness in advance. A form of praise and thanksgiving that moves the heart of God to reveal Himself to us.

Dear heavenly Father, forgive me for the times I've questioned Your intentions toward me. Help me turn my questions and murmurings into praise and worship as I wait on You. In Jesus' name. Amen.

Day 25

So you, by the help of your God, return, hold fast to love and justice, and wait continually for your God (Hosea 12:6 ESV).

Psalmist David often cried out to God, asking not to be cast away from His presence. "Take not your Holy Spirit from me. Restore to me the joy of your salvation," he wrote (Psalm 51:11-12 ESV). And God met him where he was. Sometimes our disappointment causes us to move away from the very place we need to remain—in God's arms. The chasm grows when we push Him away in our desire for what we want when we want it. And that can be a dangerous and difficult place to return from. Impatience and disappointment are deep waters that can pull us under. We find it hard to walk on the water of faith when we step out of the boat without His bidding. And yet He stands ready to draw us back to His side. We only need to call out like David did in the desert of his experience.

Know that God is on your side and will never withhold anything that is good for you. Perhaps life doesn't seem fair, but God is just. His wise counsel will prevail in your life even when you don't understand what He is doing. Call out to Him. And if you must, you can pout while in His arms. He can take it. He looks into your heart and knows how you feel anyway. With His help, you will return to a place of singing, a place of trust, a place of quietly waiting even when it feels like too much time has gone by. Allow Him to draw you to His side and then into His lap. Settle there and wait for as long as it takes. Remember, God knows best.

Dear heavenly Father, forgive me for wandering away and taking my life into my own hands. Encourage me to stay in Your arms. And when I refuse to listen, when I walk away, help me find the way back to You and the safety of life in Your arms. Be my confidence. In Jesus' name. Amen.

Day 26

To set the mind on the flesh is death, but to set the mind on the Spirit is life and peace (Romans 8:6 ESV).

Heeding the lust of the flesh, the lust of the eyes, the pride of life—feeding our unbridled desires—always leads to death. All knowledge is not good. Some of it even kills! When I allow the world to distract me with all its flashy invitations and loud conversations that rattle my spirit and leave me feeling uncertain about my life, I die in degrees. Slowly an activity or thought pattern that at one time I found appalling becomes tolerable. And as I get used to it, it births desires in me for more of what the world has to offer.

Then the discontent begins. The world looks like it is having so much fun, getting away with so much. I feel like a child who has been sent to her room. I look through the window at everyone going their own way and seeming to have so much fun.

David felt this way too on occasion. And then he stopped and considered the end result of the choices people in the world made and preferred to choose the path to God over destruction. Only when we draw close to God do we come to know firsthand that where the Spirit of the Lord is, there is liberty to experience the fulfillment we've longed for without the stress and disasters and disappointments of trying to find it the world's way. All that energy spent running after what leads to death is better conserved and used for the good things from God that lead to life and peace. As Paul said, think on the things that are lovely, of good report, of the Spirit (Philippians 4:8).

Dear heavenly Father, help me change my focus to the things that lead to life, forsaking all things that lead to death and despair. Fill and saturate me with Your Spirit that I might live fully and in peace. In Jesus' name. Amen.

⊰⊱

[The LORD said,] "Still the vision awaits its appointed time; it
hastens to the end—it will not lie. If it seems slow, wait for it;
it will surely come; it will not delay" (Habakkuk 2:3 ESV).

The difficulty in waiting for the fulfillment of our desires is that most of the time we don't know God's delivery date. And it is the not knowing, the uncertainty, that makes us crazy, that causes us to question, or that makes us try to "help" God to hasten the timing. And yet there is an appointed time for the package to arrive, for our dreams to come true.

In fact, our destiny cannot be turned back once God sets it in motion. He has anticipated every twist and turn of our lives and fits it into His elaborate schedule so that everything lines up as it should in the fullness of His timing. This is why the prophet Habakkuk encourages those who might grow discouraged. If it seems as if it is taking forever, we can rest assured that God's blessing on our desires are coming faster than we think.

I encourage you to wait patiently. Know God is active! Like a pregnant woman in her last few weeks who just wants her baby delivered, we may feel as if fulfillment is a long way out. But we know that one day our "babies" are going to be birthed. That is what labor is all about. Waiting and then pushing at just the right time under the instruction of the One who is supervising the delivery. Yes, there may be much waiting and some pain involved, but the end is beautiful, bringing life to you and those who surround you as well. And trust me, the pain of the wait will be quickly forgotten.

Dear heavenly Father, I know You are faithful to keep Your promises and deliver all good things in their perfect time. I am waiting patiently on You. In Jesus' name. Amen.

Day 28

*Whatever was written in former days was written for our instruction,
that through endurance and through the encouragement of
the Scriptures we might have hope* (Romans 15:4 ESV).

In the midst of our struggles to trust God and make peace with where we are in life right now, we need to turn to the Word of God as never before. The pages are filled with the stories of men and women like you and me who walked through the uncertainties and longings of life just like we do. They too wondered if God would show up. If their dreams would come true. If they would have the love they always dreamed of. If they would be healed, blessed, delivered. Whatever the hope, they turned to God. Their dreams and desires were beyond their ability to produce. God was and is the answer! He showed up time and time again to answer the cries of His people's hearts…and He still does.

The stories written in Scripture encourage us while we wait and give us hope. God is not a respecter of persons—what He does for one He is willing to do for all. He is seated on high, yet He hears the beats of our hearts and cheers us on, along with the cloud of witnesses who have gone before us and say "Keep the faith!"

There is hope for our lives! God is that living hope abiding in you and manifesting all you hope for in the fullness of time. Hold on a little while longer and draw strength from those who know the way you're taking because they took it first. Then dare to hope again.

*Dear heavenly Father, thank You for Your Word that is a lamp to my
feet and a constant source of encouragement. In Jesus' name. Amen.*

Day 29

"The LORD is my portion," says my soul, "therefore I will hope in him" (Lamentations 3:24 ESV).

When I finally get it that God is the One who fills—and fulfills—me, I turn my desire toward Him. Sometimes this takes a while. Can you relate? It is far easier to imagine that something we can see or touch would add so much to our world and provide concrete satisfaction. The invisible realm remains too out of reach. That is, until we draw closer to God. Close enough to feel His breath and be renewed by His Spirit. When God becomes all we hope and dream for, our wishes are answered in ways that are more deeply satisfying than we could ever hope for or imagine. When all else pales in light of who He is and what He means to me, I cease wanting. I feel restored, filled, content, happy.

God is the rewarder of those who seek Him, and He *is* the reward at the end of the day in the sense that all we seek can be and will be found in Him. All blessings begin and end with Him! Why it can take us so long to grasp this one amazing fact, and that we have to grasp it again and again, is beyond me. Perhaps it's because we're human. But there is a place where our searching ends. We come to the end of ourselves and the beginning of Him. Then we discover that He is a fabulous treasure chest filled with good things, beautiful things, things that bring us joy, peace, satisfaction, happiness, and a great sense of finally being whole.

All along God knew the plans He had for us. We just didn't. And who said surprises aren't fun?

> *Dear heavenly Father, truly You know what is best. As I finally come to the place of seeing You as You are—my rich and wonderful reward, help me share Your goodness with others so they will seek and glorify You too. In Jesus' name. Amen.*

Day 30

Surely there is a future, and your hope
will not be cut off (Proverbs 23:18 ESV).

There are few things in life we can be sure of save God is on the throne, His promises are true, and eternity waits for us all. And if we are believers and have accepted Jesus Christ as our Lord and Savior, that eternity will be glorious! And because of our faith in Him, we can rest now in the assurance that He will meet us where we are and take care of our wants and needs. He remains faithful to bring all things to pass in the fullness of His timing and make them beautiful.

As we focus on moving forward, we see brighter days because God is the Light at the end of every dark tunnel. He promises we will not be disappointed. Our hope will not be cut off because we experience Him—the reason we have hope in the first place. As His goodness unfolds in the form of the things we long for on earth, coupled with eternal blessings we can't even imagine, we become witnesses to the fact that He knew all along about everything we wonder about. His Word says as much!

As we allow His truths to sink deep into the core of our being, we are convinced we do not hope in vain. We wait with anticipation for when God will show up with the things we desire in His hands. And we'll have plenty left over to share! In this we have hope, and our joy is complete.

Dear heavenly Father, thank You for securing my future. In those times when I can't see what I long for, help me fix my gaze on You. I want to always move closer and closer to Your heart. By Your Spirit my hope will be kept alive until it manifests fully. In Jesus' name. Amen.

Day 31

The desire of the righteous ends only in good (Proverbs 11:23).

At the end of the day, Proverbs 11:23 sums up our lives in Christ. If we get what we want, it is good. If we don't get what we want, it is good too—that is, if we are righteous. If we're in that place of right-standing with God. If we've released all that we are and all that we have to Him for safekeeping. If these things are true, then we are trusting Him and the decisions He makes for us. We know that everything God does is good. Everything He does gives life. He works all out for the good of those who love the Lord and are the called according to His purpose (Romans 8:28).

Friend, are you living for God's purposes or your own? This could be where the tension is. As you release your purposes and personal agenda and choose to become part of God's kingdom agenda, you'll find that all you long for is fulfilled while fitting into His divine plan. And it's all good! No blessing is limited to just one person. A blessing becomes a joy and reminder of God's love to many as their hopes are lifted as they see God performing on behalf of His children.

I remember when a long-awaited desire of mine finally came to pass. I was amazed at how many people shared that their faith had been bolstered by watching me go through the time of waiting and the fruition of my dream in Christ.

So hope against hope, believe in the face of questions, and praise God through your laughter and tears. As you love and honor Him, He is faithful to make all things beautiful for you in His perfect timing. Wait on Him. Encourage your soul by reading His Word. Above all things, worship Him.

Dear heavenly Father, I worship You and wait on You in expectant hope. I love You. In Jesus' name. Amen.

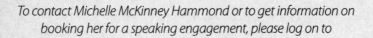

To contact Michelle McKinney Hammond or to get information on booking her for a speaking engagement, please log on to

www.michellehammond.com

A Woman's Gotta Do What a Woman's Gotta Do

Packed with upbeat stories, Michelle explores Proverbs 31 and offers intriguing questions to help you learn more about who you are and where you're going. You'll discover keys to...

- exploring and enjoying every aspect of the season of life you're in
- live up to your full potential and be who God created you to be
- have a greater, more positive impact on people around you

With enthusiasm and plenty of encouragement, Michelle offers biblical truths and valuable insights to help you grow spiritually strong and make your life more dynamic.

Right Attitudes for Right Living

Making the best choices isn't always easy. With understanding, compassion, and biblical wisdom, Michelle offers fresh perspectives, motivating affirmations, and get-it-done suggestions to help you...

- make wise choices
- live joyfully
- master your circumstances

Right Attitudes for Right Living will help you take your life to the next level to experience the extraordinary life God has planned for you.

How to Get Past Disappointment

The Samaritan woman always welcomed the heat of the sun once she sat on the edge of the well and splashed her face with cool water from the bucket she drew up. This place was her oasis of peace and refreshing. But not today. A stranger was sitting in her spot. A Jewish rabbi...

Drawing on the dramatic story of the "Woman at the Well," Michelle offers an unforgettable encounter with God to help you move beyond disappointment and experience joy. She reveals how to...

- let God's love help you face your hurts and forgive when necessary
- embrace new beginnings
- release your expectations and embrace God's blessings

You can experience God's love more fully and live the life He wants you to have.

Also available: *How to Get Past Disappointment DVD*!
Let Michelle lead your group in six dynamic, 30-minute sessions.